Borrowed Riches

Living What We Learned

Anne E. White

Borrowed Riches: Living What We Learned

Copyright © 2025 by Anne E. White www.annewrites.ca

Cover photograph and design by Anne E. White

Some portions of this book appeared first on "Archipelago," the blog of the AmblesideOnline Advisory. Other material presented elsewhere has been noted as such.

All rights reserved. No part of this publication may be reproduced, stored in a retrieval system or transmitted in any form by any means, electronic, mechanical, photocopy, recording or otherwise, without the prior permission of the publisher, except as provided by Canadian copyright law.

ISBN: 978-1-990258-34-3

Contents

Introduction: "That Noble End" 3

Nerdy, Wordy Battles 6

A Few Hazlitt Thoughts to Demonstrate That Poetry is Not a Mediaeval Torture, or a Mad Elephant 18

Each Tells Its Own Tale: The Uses of Mythology 19

Still Not Fish: The Epiphany of King Midas 35

"Even to a Boy": Lessons from Uncle Plutarch 37

Endings, Beginnings, and T. S. Eliot 49

Breaking Out of Our Raccoons 59

The Will and the Wisdom 73

Epilogue: "What Autumn Leaves Disclose" 80

Bibliography 90

For Bryan:
Bragi to my Iduna,
Philemon to my Baucis,
and Gene to my Esther

Borrowed Riches

The people of God find themselves more buoyant in the most salty seas of sorrow than in other waters. The cross does, in very deed, raise us nearer to Christ when it is fully sanctified! It could not do so if it were not sanctified by the Holy Spirit to that noble end—but under His hand it works out our lasting good. (Charles Spurgeon)

"Borrowed riches," he said smiling and catching Plato's eye. "It is the fate of the teacher, to hear his words come limping back from the pupil's mouth."

"The pupil," said Plato in that low light voice of his, "who lives what he learned, is a teacher too. A city of such pupils could teach the world."

(Mary Renault, *The Mask of Apollo*)

Introduction: "That Noble End"

On Father's Day last June, as we were getting ready for a flea market outing, my husband Bryan unexpectedly collapsed. He was rushed to the hospital but did not survive. Our family spent the rest of that day, and those that followed, in a place we did not expect to be, doing and saying things we never thought we would have to do and say, and making decisions without our decision-maker.

In Lois Lowry's novel *A Summer to Die*, the mother has been making a patchwork quilt from her girls' childhood clothing. Near the end of the book, she breaks off a thread and says, "I think it's finished. How can it be finished?" As she has recently lost a daughter, we understand that she's talking about more than the quilt. But what I also see now is that the process of making something cannot be continued indefinitely. There is joy in its completion, but there is also a sense of grief, marking both its beginnings and its ending.

I still don't know much about what grief is supposed to look like. For me, the loss of my husband was like locking the door for the final time on moving day. To be more accurate, it felt like most of the (metaphoric) furniture and household goods were left inside as well, and I found myself on the sidewalk holding only a few essentials. This has, you understand, not much to do with the actual task of sorting and disposing of lifetime possessions; it is more about life itself, past and present. What had we been watching that week in our collection of vintage shows? Who had we been praying for over morning coffee? What had we planned to make for dinner that night? Would anybody remember to water the tomatoes? In just one day, those things became someone else's life, a quilt no longer attached to the stitching frame. And before much more time had passed, I made the decision to move to an apartment, which meant letting go of even more things from our shared life, and acquiring different ones. (I did water the tomatoes.)

What does any of this, a purely personal story of life events, have to do with a book about Charlotte Mason's educational philosophy, with thoughts about words, choices and will? Perhaps nothing, perhaps everything. I have my current experience of salty seas, you have yours. But there is something I want to share about the man my husband was, and who he was becoming, that goes beyond the simply personal memories, the hobbies and quirks and fondness for hotdogs. He was a lifelong learner who could remember, it seemed, whole filing-cabinets full of information about anything that interested him, and who was willing to learn something new from just about anyone, from a Messianic evangelist to the guy asking for money outside the coffee shop. I recently heard a tribute to a particular American, saying he believed in "conversation that would heal," and that he was able to talk about his beliefs "in a way that was kind." That was also Bryan. If you made a word cloud of the things people posted and said about him, the words "gentle" and "kind" would be at the top, with "funny" close behind. He often had the garage door open when he painted or cleaned or fixed things, and on those days a stream of neighbours would stop while dog-walking or going to the store, sometimes just for a minute, sometimes longer, and share what was on their minds. (Bryan was a good listener, but the one thing he was not always good at was remembering names, so I often heard about "the man with the golden retriever," or "the couple carrying big ice-capps.") When he went to pick up a vintage stereo receiver or turntable at someone's house (or they came to our garage for the same), a few minutes' stop could turn into an hour. Even grumpy clerks at service counters would often be won over by his talent for trying to make it a better day instead of a worse one.

It wasn't that Bryan didn't worry or get stressed. He had what Miss Stacy called his "own little set of troubles." But he also had prayer, and trust, and Star Trek, and classic cars, and bowling shirts, and a life that exemplified the wide room and the science of relations. I was privileged to have a front-row seat on all of that for over thirty years; it is, indeed, my quilt of memories. But, again, what relevance might this have for those who never knew him?

I would like to direct your attention to a tribute to Charlotte Mason, written by another educator, Mr. H. W. Household. It says, in part:

> Her face was full of light, of wide sympathy and understanding, of delicate humour and gentleness and love. When she talked with you she brought out the best that was in you, something that you did not know was there...Though she taught a new thing, a new way, and in teaching had to show the old things and the old ways for what they really are, her criticism left no sting. She could not be anything but

Introduction: "That Noble End"

> generous and the ways of her mind were wide. (*The Story of Charlotte Mason*, p. 134)

Mason herself similarly paid tribute to another friend and educator, Thomas Godolphin Rooper (it is the final chapter of her book *Formation of Character*):

> All who worked with him had the assurance that if there were a defect he would see it, and would help to mend it.

And a few pages later, after praising Mr. Rooper's intelligence, wisdom, and serious devotion to his work, she takes a different note:

> He was incapable of pettiness or ungentle criticism; and whether his audiences were small and dull, large and intellectual, or large and fashionable, he always seemed to take the same gleeful delight that such an audience (of whichever sort) should gather for the consideration of an educational topic...It is difficult to speak of Mr. Rooper's delightful and stimulating conversation, and of his genial interest in everything. We have lost a great man, and at a moment apparently when his achievements, his gifts and his knowledge should have been of special value to the nation he served. (pp. 425–428)

Glee and delight. Interest in everything. Bringing out the best in people. Generosity in its deepest and most chivalric sense. These are the words we should all want to have spoken of us, not only by those closest to us, but by the people at service counters, the visitors at church coffee hour, and the neighbours with dogs (even if we can't pin down their names). All this is what we are aiming at in a Charlotte Mason education.

It's now the middle of October, and the tomatoes, though watered, are finished. I'm making dinner in a new apartment oven, with groceries brought in from a different supermarket, and I'm looking out at an interesting but much-changed view of the city (and now with autumn colour appearing as well). The novelty of it all is, perhaps, adding a certain buoyancy to these salty seas. Even storm clouds can have their own beauty, especially when viewed from the shelter of an upper-floor balcony. "Under His hand it works out our lasting good."

Come in and let's talk about Norse myths and C. S. Lewis, Emerson and Plutarch, T. S. Eliot, and neighbours with potatoes.

Nerdy, Wordy Battles

Some years ago, I was at a homeschool conference and got into a discussion with a vendor of books for conservative families. She earnestly suggested that I trade in *Peter Rabbit* for a book about "real rabbits," of which I am sure there were many lovely examples, but the point is that *Peter Rabbit* is equally a real rabbit, or, more so, a real character. As C. S. Lewis wrote in *A Preface to "Paradise Lost"*, "Even Peter Rabbit came to grief because he *would* go into Mr. McGregor's garden." Peter's desires and his disobedience very much mirror our own. And yet there is no need to hammer all that home when we read the story to a child; it is simply there along with the bread and milk and blackberries.

Lewis wrote elsewhere that books and music are not the thing in themselves, they are "only" a means through which we are given a longing for things beyond ourselves, "only the scent of a flower we have not found, the echo of a tune we have not heard, news from a country we have never yet visited" (*The Weight of Glory*). In our time and place, the means, the "only," is exactly what we do have to begin with, and it may be all we will have for quite a long time to come. But even scents and echoes can teach us a great deal.

> Other echoes
> Inhabit the garden. Shall we follow?
> Quick, said the bird, find them, find them,
> Round the corner.
>
> (T. S. Eliot, "Burnt Norton" in *Four Quartets*)

Sticking with Words

Philip Yancey says that God revealed himself not through graphic images or idols, but "in the most freedom-enhancing way imaginable: through words." For Yancey, that's a good enough reason to keep "sticking with words" ("Why I Write"). Most Charlotte Mason educators do not need convincing of the value of words.

However, the further we go on, the more reassurance we may need that our enthusiasm for words is not futile and exhausting, or in some

Nerdy, Wordy Battles

way even harmful to our listeners—or to ourselves. We find ourselves running into Hamlet's "Words, words, words." Or quotes such as this, from Alan Jacobs' book *The Narnian*:

> Words are tokens of the will. If something stronger
> than language were available, then we would use it.

Or passages such as this one, from C. S. Lewis's novel *Till We Have Faces*. The main character Orual, speaking from her lifetime of bitterness, insists that:

> When the time comes to you at which you will be
> forced at last to utter the speech which has lain at
> the center of your soul for years, which you have, all
> that time, idiot-like, been saying over and over,
> you'll not talk about joy of words.

We may even come across Bible verses such as 1 Timothy 1:6, which J. B. Phillips translates as "Some seem to have forgotten [genuine faith] and to have lost themselves in endless words." The author of those letters later reminds his readers "not to fight wordy battles, which help no one and may undermine the faith of some who hear them" (2 Timothy 2:14, Phillips).

Are those the same "words" that Philip Yancey describes as "freedom-enhancing?"

Kind of. Sort of. As Jacobs says, words are just the tokens, the tools; or perhaps a better analogy would be the nails rather than the hammer. But let's not blame the nails for how they're pounded in.

In the passage above from *The Narnian*, Jacobs is describing a period in the life of C. S. Lewis in which he seemed to fear "that he would come to trust too much in his own powers or argument and persuasion." He knew he was almost too good an arguer on many subjects, including (and particularly) Christian apologetics. He once said, "No doctrine of the Faith seems to me so spectral, so unreal as one that I have just *successfully* defended in a public debate." And yet again, perhaps it wasn't the words (or the nails) themselves, as much as a certain lack of joy over the tasks Lewis was now expected to carry out as an acknowledged voice for Christianity. He recognized the need to defend truth and beauty, but he found the battles into which he was drafted somehow hollow, "unreal," even self-defeating. Jacobs points out that, in Lewis's own conversion experience,

> Arguments had cleared away many of his [own] philosophical objections to Christianity, but even when those objections disappeared he could not move forward into actual belief...until he had acquired a positive vision of a *story* that he could inhabit...He became a Christian not through accepting a particular set of arguments but through learning to read a story the right way.

Perhaps that was a reason why, Lewis, in the last decade or so of his life, turned to writing fiction. And not just any fiction, but fairy tales. Not, we must quickly insert here, as a sort of false front or propaganda, but as something vital and "freedom-enhancing." Not empty words such as those that Orual repeats in *Till We Have Faces*, but life-giving ones. Not just an argument, but a story. Not something less real, but more so. A story, a place, a world, that the reader can inhabit. We need to keep pushing through those fur coats in the wardrobe, until we see glimmerings of Narnian snow and lantern light.

> Every time we use words, we're either fighting against [mob mentality] or giving in to it. When we fight against it, we're taking the side of genuine and permanent human civilization. (Northrop Frye, *The Educated Imagination*)

But what if we need something even more counter-intuitive than fiction? Like...poetry?

You Knew There Was Going to Be a Mitford Reference, So Here It Is Already

The penultimate novel in Jan Karon's *Mitford* series, *To Be Where You Are*, opens with Father Tim attempting to make an osteoporosis-fighting smoothie in a vintage blender. He drops in several hard-to-pronounce ingredients, adds lumps of frozen fruit, and then almost kills the motor trying to blend it all together.

> When the nurse gave him the recipe after his physical, she didn't say the ingredients had to be thawed. He did not have time to wait for something to thaw. He hit Blend again. A sound like tires screaming on a NASCAR track.

Nerdy, Wordy Battles

Later, his wife Cynthia is told she also needs to build up her bones, so she tries the same recipe, also with mixed (or unmixed) results. (At the end of the book, there's a gift-of-the-Magi moment when they each give the other a new blender for Christmas.) This plot thread about blender drinks, cardio walks, and cutting out coffee (Father Tim loves his coffee) may seem minor in a novel where a lot of other things happen (well, as much as ever happens in Mitford); but pay attention, there's an analogy coming up.

The early 20th-century writer Arnold Bennett insists, in his book *How to Live on 24 Hours a Day*, that reading poetry, and *about* poetry, should be, so to speak, our calcium-loaded smoothie for the mind. Bennett also likes history and philosophy, but he thinks poetry is more accessible for beginners. His reason for skipping fiction isn't that it is unreal or immoral, but rather that even excellent novels move too quickly to give an effective reading workout. They are, so to speak, almost too much fun, and go down too easily. Bennett thinks we should get more mind exercise by reading something full of acai berries, tahini, and almond milk—even if we can't get it all blended.

> She tried again. 'There's a blob of something in here.'
>
> 'I think there's supposed to be a blob or two.'
>
> 'But a smoothie is supposed to be smooth.'
>
> 'Blobs are good for you.' It was his final argument.
>
> (*To Be Where You Are*)

Bennett's first prescription is the 1818 essay "On Poetry in General," by the painter / philosopher / essayist William Hazlitt. He explains why:

> It is the best thing of its kind in English, and no one who has read it can possibly be under the misapprehension that poetry is a mediaeval torture, or a mad elephant, or a gun that will go off by itself and kill at forty paces. Indeed, it is difficult to imagine the mental state of the man who, after reading Hazlitt's essay, is not urgently desirous of reading some poetry before his next meal.

Five-star review, obviously. However, like a tall glass of Father Tim's not-so-smoothie, we may find Hazlitt's fifteen or so pages not only overwhelming, but full of things we don't even recognize. Here are a few of the not too difficult blobs:

> Poetry is the universal language which the heart holds with nature and itself.
>
> If history is a grave study, poetry may be said to be a graver: its materials lie deeper, and are spread wider...It is not a branch of authorship: it is 'the stuff of which our life is made'. The rest is 'mere oblivion', a dead letter: for all that is worth remembering in life, is the poetry of it.
>
> The child is a poet in fact, when he first plays at hide-and-seek, or repeats the story of Jack the Giant-killer; the shepherd-boy is a poet, when he first crowns his mistress with a garland of flowers; the countryman when he stops to look at the rainbow; the city-apprentice, when he gazes after the Lord Mayor's show; the miser, when he hugs his gold...
>
> If poetry is a dream, the business of life is much the same. If it is a fiction, made up of what we wish things to be, and fancy that they are, because we wish them so, there is no other nor better reality.

Bennett is not insisting that you fall in love with Hazlitt's Romantic-era writing; neither is he suggesting that an essay on poetry can replace the real thing. But as you drink it in, it can help to build up your confidence and understanding of its possibilities. Hazlitt, of course, is not the only good poetry resource; there are books, essays, classes and podcasts and videos. We are, truly, embarrassed by riches. But who else but Hazlitt is going to cover not only the Bible, Homer, Dante, *Robinson Crusoe*, and John Bunyan in one essay, but also introduce you to Ossian? He's worth at least sampling.

Back in Mitford, Father Tim and Cynthia are also prescribed a thrice-weekly "cardio walk" around town. Bennett's version of that is to read some narrative poetry, such as Elizabeth Barrett Browning's novel-length poem *Aurora Leigh*. His advice:

> Forget that it is fine poetry. Read it simply for the story and the social ideas. And when you have done, ask yourself honestly whether you still dislike poetry.

Notice that Bennett offers us only the "means through which we are given a longing." Only the only. The images, the scents, the echoes. He may have a whole shelf of other favourite books, but we don't need to know about them, at least not yet. We need to try making word smoothies for ourselves—even if they look like nothing our blender has ever seen before.

(I have only ever had a couple of real smoothies, and they were overpriced ones at airport coffee shops, an indulgence after surviving body-and-soul-depleting security lines. But last week I happened to have the remains of a deli baby-kale-fruit salad in the fridge, along with a banana and a bit of yogurt, so I devised the cunning plot of turning it all into a smoothie. I dumped everything into my (not-too-powerful) blender and whizzed away. Result: ground-up baby kale coated with fruit. I added some milk and tried again. Result: liquid ground-up baby kale coated with fruit. Well, I did drink as much of it as I could. But I'm sharing just so you know that when I say that results aren't always great the first time, I know what I'm talking about.)

How Do the Poets Feel About That?

Do you have a favourite Christian poet?
Should we stop there?
A couple of years ago, some of us were reviewing possible additions to the AmblesideOnline Curriculum, including an anthology of American Christian poets. We ended up not using it, not just because some of the poems went a bit darker than we wanted, but more, I think, because the scattered poems in the anthology felt like the authors had been slapped with name tags reading "Hi, My Name Is Christian Poet (And Stop Calling Me Religious)." Deciding who the Christian poets are, or what they should write, is one problem; but getting people to read them is another.

In 1976, Rod Jellema wrote an essay for *Christianity Today* titled "Poems Should Stay Across the Street from the Church." Jellema's big question was this (he used it as a subheading): "Are Christians Really Serious About Poetry?" His feeling was, not so much. But that they should be. And not just about Christian poetry, but all good poetry. Which would, I'm sure, have absolutely freaked out the Peter Rabbit lady.

Here are a few ways that Jellema describes poetry:

> "Poems...get us beyond understanding into layer upon layer of the exact feel of 'thingness...'"

> "The poet's job is to catch, discover, reveal..."

> "The imagination rides out the play that can exist among words and images until it makes a living body that shows and is but 'cannot be said.'"

> "[Poetry] is the process of its own little discovery: it leaves its footprints; the reader can follow the creative process step by step, feeling the swerves and leaps and undertones and soundings and strange connections in the language that got the poet's imagination into that unified awareness, that little incarnation, the poem."

And then he makes an interesting point: "The Church and the poets do not have much in common just now. But they probably do share one deep conviction: that our basic needs lie far, far beneath the search for the mere social machinery of problem-solving."

> Society, by degrees, is constructed into a machine that carries us safely and insipidly from one end of life to the other, in a very comfortable prose style. (Hazlitt, "On Poetry in General")

In other words: we need each other.

And, in a word to poets who are Christian, Jellema warns that they have no right to dump articles of faith into verse and call it done:

> The problem with those heady doctrines is that I can mumble them. And what I can mumble, the poem cannot incorporate or believe...I got to my own position, not by reading all those ponderous works about the relations between art and Christianity, but by trying to keep the poems honestly poems. Only now, thinking it out on paper and dipping into those works, do I discover that it's pretty much the solution of others, too. Eliot and Auden, for example.

(Which might affirm the value of narration in education. One way to describe it, maybe, is that we learn not to mumble.)

I think Rod Jellema (in his 1976 lament) would have been

encouraged by the existence and persistence today of poets who profess(ed) Christian faith and are read by a wide audience: Wendell Berry, Mary Oliver, Dana Gioia, and Malcolm Guite, to name just a few. He would surely have been pleased by the appearance of creative hubs such as the Rabbit Room in Tennessee; by the popularity of literature-themed podcasts; and by the growth of self-publishing and other online opportunities to showcase old and new poetry. What he might have continued to ask, though, is: are even the poets I named, and also those of younger generations, known and welcome in churches today? And what about poetry that is less obviously, or not at all, "Christian?" Do Christians still want poetry and other forms of art to stay across the road? Do they even care enough to have the conversation?

In the 1973 Billy Graham movie *Time to Run* (something that many of us over a certain age watched at church, usually on a creaky 16mm projector), part of the story is based on Francis Thompson's 1890 poem "The Hound of Heaven." The possible identity of "the hound"—a mysterious entity that pursues the narrator of the poem—is discussed in a college class, and then the subject keeps coming up between the main character and his girlfriend, who is irritating him by hanging out with the Jesus People in the park and listening to Randy Stonehill songs. My point is simply that, in 1973, college students and hippies (and Billy Graham) knew how to groove to Thompson's

> I stand amid the dust o' the mounded years—
>
> My mangled youth lies dead beneath the heap.
>
> My days have crackled and gone up in smoke,
>
> Have puffed and burst as sun-starts on a stream

as much they did to Stonehill's "I love you I love you I love you." Fifty-plus years later, though? I'm not so sure.

From the Ground Up

> ...Education is a matter of developing the intellect and the imagination, which deal with reality, and reality is always irrelevant. (*Northrop Frye in Conversation*)
>
> ...all that is worth remembering in life, is the poetry

of it...there is no other nor better reality. (Hazlitt, "On Poetry in General")

Are poets and literary critics just being cute when they say that imagination and poetry are more real than the everyday world?

In *Time to Run*, the main character rejects his parents' bourgeois lifestyle and runs away; but, like the biblical prodigal son, he eventually finds himself washing cars to survive. That's a slap in the face kind of reality. But in the meantime, his parents are struggling with their science-and-technology version of reality, one that pays for the nice house and the college tuition but leaves something lacking. The father's colleague, confronted by one of the Jesus People, says flatly, "I believe in what works." But what does?

You may have heard before that the word "poetry" is rooted in the Greek words *poiesis,* the act of creation, and *poiema,* the creation, something that is made (also translated "workmanship"). Poetry is something that both speaks of God's creative nature and reflects our own. Could we say, then, that Creation is the ultimate "what works?" And the final "more real?" But we have to find our own place in that reality; our own "bit of the world's work" (to quote Charlotte Mason); or, perhaps even more, our bit of the world's poetry.

A few years ago, I was speaking at the L'HaRMaS retreat in Kingsville, Ontario, on the topic of the Arts and Crafts movement. I mentioned Lloyd Alexander's novel *Taran Wanderer*, where the young hero Taran is going through a major identity crisis, mainly because he's in love with Princess Eilonwy, and as an orphaned assistant pig keeper, he doesn't feel he's worthy of her, so he sets out on a journey to find out who he is. He meets a metalsmith named Hevydd and persuades him to teach him his craft. Hevydd puts Taran to work digging fuel for the fire and smelting rocks, which just about kills him. Finally, Taran is allowed to make a sword, and he thinks it's beautiful and perfect, but when he strikes it hard, it falls to pieces. So, what then? He starts all over, and his second sword is not as pretty, but it's much stronger, and Hevydd says, "Yours it is, more than any other, for you forged it with your own hands."

Hevydd offers him the chance to stay and finish his apprenticeship, but Taran decides he needs to move on. He meets a weaver who says she will teach him to weave a cloak, but, just like the smith, she makes him start by picking burrs out of wool and spinning thread. After a long effort, Taran ends up with a decent cloak, but he doesn't want to stay and be a weaver either. Since fairy tale things always come in threes, he then has a similar experience with a potter. Each craftsperson gives Taran a different metaphor of life: the smith tells him that life is a forge that hammers us into shape, the weaver says that it is a loom in which we are weaving a pattern, and the potter says that life moulds us like clay.

When I first spoke about that passage, I was trying to make the point that we begin with beginnings; that knowledge and skill will come, but it takes patience and faith to continue when success seems elusive. But now I am reading it like this: that in our search for "what works," we may be rescued both by poetry (in its wider, deeper sense of "making") and by the Poet. We hear that reality in nonsense songs and hymns of praise, in laughter and lament. We see it while peering through a small hole cut in cardboard and writing down what we see. We feel it when our hands hold a paintbrush, a crochet hook, a lump of clay, a mixing spoon, a guitar, even a screwdriver or soldering iron. We experience it when we restore something dusty and decrepit. We know it in the ancient tasks of naming, and of teaching those names. As Hazlitt says, the "poetry" of speaking, of singing, of making, of reassembling (some call that metaphor), may be all that is worth remembering from our lives on this earth.

It is what works. It is what's real. And it's what connects us to the Realest of the Real.

Going Deeper with Mr. Hazlitt

> Poetry is in all its shapes the **language** of the imagination and the passions, of fancy and will. Nothing, therefore, can be more absurd than the outcry which has been sometimes raised by frigid and pedantic critics, for reducing the **language** of poetry to the standard of common sense and reason: for the end and use of poetry, 'both at the first and now, was and is to hold the mirror up to nature', seen through the medium of passion and imagination, not divested of that medium by means of literal truth or abstract reason.
>
> The painter of history might as well be required to represent the face of a person who has just trod

> upon a serpent with the still-life expression of a common portrait, as the poet to describe the most striking and vivid impressions which things can be supposed to make upon the mind, in the **language** of common conversation... the impressions of common sense and strong imagination, that is, of passion and indifference, cannot be the same, and **they must have a separate language** to do justice to either. (Hazlitt)

In Hazlitt's day, there was apparently an attempt to reduce language to a literal, "common sense" character, or, on the other hand, to the extremely abstract (and therefore almost meaningless). Nerdy, wordy battles are obviously not only a phenomenon of our own time. If poetry is meant to "hold the mirror up to nature" (a line from Hamlet as well as Hazlitt), we can only see into that mirror through a "medium of passion and imagination." What could that mean?

In his book *Why Literature Still Matters*, Jason M. Baxter begins with a comparison of two pieces of writing: a letter from Mark Zuckerberg and Priscilla Chan, addressed to their infant daughter; and the poem "A Prayer for My Daughter," by William Butler Yeats. Baxter reads Zuckerberg's letter to the college students he teaches, and he says that, though full of philanthropic thoughts, it gets only a "tepid, guarded response...They know that Zuckerberg and Chan are saying 'The Right Things,' but for some reason they don't feel moved by what they hear." There's not much to disagree with; but there's not much to care about, either.

I can't cover the full comparison here, but, briefly, Baxter says that Yeats, in writing *his* poem, "reaches down within and stirs up the embers of his heart." Then there is this, which Hazlitt would have appreciated: "Clearly, the way of Yeats is not scientific...[he] does not primarily see the natural world as a set of resources which need to be mined, analyzed, pulled to pieces, and rebuilt into more useful things...[watch this now] Rather, the natural world's chief value is found when it is 'looked upon,' loved, internalized, and then re-spoken, or painted or played or prayed." Looked upon, loved, internalized, and...narrated? And with the passion of a parent who has just trod on a plastic building brick first thing in the morning, with inspiring language stirred up from the embers of the heart.

Malcolm Guite's poem "The Singing Bowl" is about a song born

Nerdy, Wordy Battles

from "This moment's pulse, this rhythm in your blood." Heart, pulse, blood, bone-building, bruised feet—we keep coming back to the same physical imagery. Baxter says that we need to love and internalize the natural world, which includes our own selves; but we also require language to allow that to happen. That doesn't mean fancy vocabulary, but honest, thoughtful, blood-and-bones words. Some wonderful poetry uses simple language. Some of it is even written by children.

> Tree-toad is never seen
> Unless a star squeezes through the leaves,
> Or a moth looks sharply at a gray branch.
> How would it be, I wonder,
> To sing patiently all night,
> Never thinking that people are asleep?
>
> (Hilda Conkling)

Should we exchange this bit of fancy, as the conference vendor might have suggested, for a book on the life cycle of tree-toads? Certainly not. But if we are beginning from that barren place, as many of us are—as many children are—we must do whatever we can to stir up the embers of our hearts. How to do this? One, refuse to read mumbling work masquerading as literature. Two, make poetry smoothies, even if your blender can't quite handle the bits and chunks. (And hope that you get a new blender for Christmas.)

> Poetry is not irregular lines in a book, but
> something very close to dance and song, something
> to walk down the street keeping time to. (Northrop
> Frye, *The Educated Imagination*)

Borrowed Riches

A Few Hazlitt Thoughts to Demonstrate That Poetry is Not a Mediaeval Torture, or a Mad Elephant

[Poetry is] to take the language of the imagination from off the ground, and enable it to spread its wings where it may indulge its own impulses...It is to common language, what springs are to a carriage, or wings to feet.

[Imaginative] language is not the less true to nature, because it is false in point of fact; but so much the more true and natural, if it conveys the impression which the object under the influence of passion makes on the mind...

[Here's one for Charlotte Mason.] Impassioned poetry is an emanation of the moral and intellectual part of our nature, as well as of the sensitive—of the desire to know, the will to act, and the power to feel; and ought to appeal to these different, parts of our constitution, in order to be perfect.

[And here's one for the AO Curriculum.] If it is of the essence of poetry to strike and fix the imagination, whether we will or no, to make the eye of childhood glisten with the starting tear, to be never thought of afterwards with indifference, John Bunyan and Daniel Defoe may be permitted to pass for poets in their way.

Each Tells Its Own Tale: The Uses of Mythology

Adapted from a talk given at L'HaRMaS, October 2025.

This talk was first written for "Set Your Feet," which takes place every July, and which is, as I understand it, L'HaRMaS in Ohio. The organizers had asked me to come and speak there this summer, and because I had been writing study guides for the AmblesideOnline mythology books, and reading and thinking a lot about mythology, I planned to talk about why it should be a key part of a Charlotte Mason education. After a great deal of messing around with flights between Toronto and Cleveland, I finally had my travel plans set, and I thought my biggest worry was going to be making sure my cell phone worked in the U.S. As some of you already know, my life changed drastically right then, as my husband passed away, and those travel plans were put on hold. But I still planned on coming to Kingsville in October, and I hoped that some of what I had prepared to say in Ohio would work here as well.

So, with all that going on, you might wonder why there is nothing more personal in this, no stories about what I've walked through over the past several months. I can only refer to the writer Katherine Paterson's story about not getting any valentines in the first grade. Years later her mother asked why she didn't write a story about that, and she said, "*All* my stories are about the time I didn't get any valentines" (*Gates of Excellence*). So, it's all in there, if you listen for it. But in the meantime, let's talk about some stories from the storehouse.

I'm basing this on one of my favourite chapters in Charlotte Mason's *Parents and Children*, with the somewhat daunting title "A Scheme of Educational Theory Proposed to Parents." I'll read what you might call the sermon text, which starts on page 231:

> Once more, we know that there is a storehouse of thought wherein we may find all the great ideas that have moved the world. We are above all things anxious to give the child the key to this storehouse…

Borrowed Riches

> We are determined that the children shall love books, therefore we do not interpose ourselves between the book and the child. We read him his *Tanglewood Tales*, and when he is a little older his *Plutarch*, not trying to break up or water down, but leaving the child's mind to deal with the matter as it can.
> (*Parents and Children*, pp. 231–232)

We all have pictures in our minds of the first things we ever saw. We remember a shell or a seagull on the beach, a song somebody was singing to us, a thunderstorm, the light coming through a coloured window in church, or the taste of a tomato from the garden.

Maybe we remember going to the beach and sitting on the sand with a shovel and a pail, as someone showed us how to dig a hole just deep enough to let the water come up. We had no idea how that could happen, but we dug another hole, and—look at that, the water came up in that one too. But when we went back home and dug in the sandbox or the garden, we could dig holes all day, and no water came up—why was that? Even if we poured water in the hole, it just went away and left mud, though the mud could also be interesting.

If we lived on a farm with chickens, we learned early on that more eggs appeared every morning, though we didn't know how that happened. Or maybe we lived in a city apartment, and our daily magic included getting into the box called an elevator, and out of it again, and suddenly we were in a different place. Being very small in a very big world is like the beginning of Mary Oliver's poem "The Summer Day":

> Who made the world?
>
> Who made the swan, and the black bear?
>
> Who made the grasshopper?
>
> This grasshopper, I mean—
>
> The one who has flung herself out of the grass,
>
> The one who is eating sugar out of my hand,
>
> who is moving her jaws back and forth instead of up and down...

But as we grew, we learned more names for things; we noticed differences and put things in groups; and we asked questions about how things work. Eventually we may have learned so much about one or more of those things that we became entitled to call ourselves scientists or composers, or economists, or theologians. But if we were lucky, we were also able to keep our early sense of interest and wonder and awe about it all.

Now, many of us here will call ourselves Charlotte Mason homeschoolers or educators. Most Charlotte Mason educators can recite the motto of the PNEU, which is "I am, I can, I ought, I will." We can name the three instruments of learning ("an atmosphere, a discipline, a life"). We may even be able to rhyme off quite a few of her educational principles. However, I think it's fair to say that few of us, if any, know what Mason called the "stages of educational intimacy," in her book *School Education*, starting on page 76. She writes:

> His parents know that the first step in intimacy is **recognition**; and they will measure his education, not solely by his progress in the 'three R's,' but by the number of living and growing things he knows by look, name, and habitat… **Aesthetic appreciation** follows close upon recognition, for does he not try from very early days to catch the flower in its beauty of colour and grace of gesture with his own paintbrush?…**First-hand Knowledge.**—By-and-by he passes from acquaintance, the pleasant recognition of friendly faces, to knowledge, the sort of knowledge we call science… All the time he is storing up associations of delight which will come back for his refreshment when he is an old man. With this sort of **appreciative knowledge** of things to begin with, the superstructure of **exact knowledge**, living science, no mere affair of text-books and examinations, is easily raised, because a natural desire is implanted. (pp. 76–78, bolds mine)

The important point is this: that every sort of knowledge must begin at its beginning, with the chance to look for oneself, to wonder, to touch, to sort, to stop and listen.

This talk is, officially, about how and why Charlotte Mason and the Parents' Union taught mythology to young students. But to get there, we have to begin with nature study, and I'll explain why. If we open *Parents and Children* to page 231, to just before the part about the storehouse, we read this: "Thus our first thought with regard to Nature-knowledge is that the child should have a living personal acquaintance with the things he sees." When we see that word "thus," we know we need to find out what comes before or after it, and the pages just before that are all about *ideas*. For instance:

> The object of lessons should be in the main twofold: to train a child in certain mental habits, [such] as attention, accuracy, promptness, etc., and to nourish him with ideas which may bear fruit in his life…Every habit has its beginning. The beginning is the idea, which comes with a stir and takes possession of us. (pp. 229-230)

So, we have the image of something stirring inside us, ideas possessing us, something like a baby growing inside the mother that begins to move and kick, to make itself known. We have Ideas. We have Nature-knowledge. And those two begin to combine, to blend into each other. We let children see the things around them, the things of the earth and the sky and the ocean, in their living context. We take them to places where they can see what comes and goes through the days, the seasons, and the years. We teach them what to call the pinecones, horse chestnuts, and black walnuts on the ground; how to name the orioles, chickadees and cardinals they hear in the trees, and tell those sounds from those of frogs and squirrels. This is the first stage, "the pleasant recognition of friendly faces."

We may complain that it's hard to make even this much happen, because many of us are not "nature people." Yes, it takes effort. But here's the good part: this is not an in-your-face, memorize vocabulary lists, fill out this worksheet and have a quiz on it kind of learning, but a "seed to the mind," a first-ideas relationship, powered by curiosity but also by reverence and humility. Mason writes, "…let words convey

Each Tells Its Own Tale

ideas as he is able to bear them. Buttercup, primrose, dandelion, magpie, each tells its own tale..." (*Parents and Children*, p. 77).

To use a different analogy, we are not raising the evil Sid in the movie *Toy Story*, who likes getting new toys only so he can deconstruct them; or the chicken man thief in the sequel who wants vintage toys so he can sell them to a museum. We want our children to be more like Bonnie, the little girl in *Toy Story 3*, who finds Woody the Cowboy lying on the ground and takes him home to have fun with. And if Bonnie had been old enough to read, she might have noticed the first owner's name Sharpied on the bottom of Woody's boot. That, too, is part of *our* discovery of the world, seeing the creator's signature in unexpected places.

This is a gift for us as well as for our children. It can be a challenge, but it's not meant to be a burden. Think of it as a picnic basket that you can hardly wait to unpack; or something that was back-ordered so long ago that you almost forgot about it. Or a jar of strawberry-rhubarb jam that your grandma made, sealed with paraffin, labelled with ballpoint pen on masking tape, that you've been saving for a special day. There's a sense of anticipation while you open it up, and then you want to take a picture or tell somebody that the package is here; or phone up grandma to say how good the jam is.

So, back to that page in *Parents and Children*. After the part about nature study, there's a bit about "object lessons," warning that a thing being examined can become less important than the teacher's list of questions about it, so that we miss the actual thing-ness of that thing. If that sounds confusing, don't worry, we'll come back to it.

And then we turn a sharp corner, with a paragraph headed "We trust much to Good Books," which is the literary equivalent of pinecones and chickadees. Mason says here, very simply, "We read him his *Tanglewood Tales*, and when he is a little older his Plutarch." She does not list a hundred books there, or even ten, but just two. Why those two? Was she randomly tossing off a couple of titles, that could just as easily have been "We read him his *Tale of Peter Rabbit*, and when he is older his *Peter Pan*?" I don't think so, though those are also good books. She seems to have chosen those two deliberately, and, just as the pinecone makes more sense when you find it under its own tree, we need to keep her context in mind.

And, in fact, Mason makes it very clear now what she's up to. We are to bring the children along with us on a walk, a journey, a "long explore" through the best ideas. We want them to begin with those ideas wherever they can, to work through the stages of recognition and aesthetic appreciation before they worry about first-hand and exact knowledge; without breaking it up into pieces, like an object lesson, or watering it down, like a lecture or a workbook page. And we want them to discover the creator's name written throughout the story.

So, we must ask again, how did *Tanglewood Tales* and Plutarch's *Lives* make this very small, very particular cut? Why did Mason view those two books as equivalent to a child excitedly telling about something he has seen on a walk?

Tanglewood Tales

In 1851, the American writer Nathaniel Hawthorne was becoming well known for his short stories and novels, such as *The Scarlet Letter* and *The House of the Seven Gables*. In the spring of that year, he began adapting a few classical myths into a book for children, titled *A Wonder Book for Girls and Boys*. He wrote to his publisher, "Unless I greatly mistake, these old fictions will work up admirably for the purpose… of course, I shall purge out all the old heathen wickedness, and put in a moral wherever practicable." The Hawthorne children said later on that, as their father had practiced the stories on them so many times, they "could repeat much of the book by heart before it was in the printer's hands." Bedtime stories are very important!

Hawthorne had planned to start writing *Tanglewood Tales*, the sequel, during the summer of 1852, but that was the year that another friend, Franklin Pierce, asked him to write a biography during his presidential campaign. However, Hawthorne found time to work on *Tanglewood* the next winter, and by March he was rushing it off to his publisher. He bragged a bit about the stories, saying, "They are done up in excellent style, purified from all moral stains, re-created as good as new, or better, and fully equal, in their own way, to Mother Goose. I never did anything else so well as these old baby stories." He was correct, at least, that the stories would be well accepted. He did not make a great deal of money from them, but the two volumes together became one of the classic retellings of children's mythology.

To clear up any confusion about Mason's mention just of the

second book, *Tanglewood Tales*, there was a popular British edition which combined stories from both books under that title, so that's probably the one she was most familiar with. And, if we ask why she mentioned Hawthorne, if she preferred his retellings over somebody else's: well, we know that by the 1920's, the PNEU term programmes regularly scheduled Andrew Lang's 1907 book *Tales of Troy and Greece*, or, as a second option, Charles Lamb's *Adventures of Ulysses*, which had been published a hundred years before that, so obviously it wasn't a case of wanting either older or newer titles in the curriculum. I think the real intention was to direct children, early on, into the storehouse room marked "Mythology," and to offer them there a whole picnic lunch, not broken into "little bits of everything" (p. 231), but in as large and meaty a portion as possible, no matter which book was used.

How does that line up with Hawthorne's claim to be "purging out all the old heathen wickedness," or his choice to cast Pandora and Epimetheus as children rather than adults? Are we contradicting ourselves by recommending a "chicken-nuggets" version of an adult tale? (Maybe we should just skip mythology until they're older.) In one of Hawthorne's framing stories, young Eustace Bright, the fictional narrator, is criticized for that exact thing, so we will let Eustace defend himself:

> "I described the giant as he appeared to me," replied the student, rather piqued. "And, sir, if you would only bring your mind into such a relation with these fables as is necessary in order to remodel them, you would see at once that an old Greek had no more exclusive right to them than a modern Yankee has. They are the common property of the world, and of all time."

This is exactly Mason's point about the "keys to the storehouse." Hawthorne's stories, even if he "remodeled" them somewhat, are still the real deal, the "vital matter." They contain themes that we begin to recognize in childhood and keep learning throughout our lives: for instance, that getting your wish can go terribly wrong; that curiosity can be dangerous; or that a simple life of love and hospitality brings its own rewards. These stories have something genuine about them that makes us tearful, or joyful, or thoughtful, long afterwards. They do not necessarily have to be *useful* in a sense of checking off cultural or literary awareness boxes. As parents and teachers, we like *useful*. If we're asked why we're reading mythology, we may say that knowing about Zeus and Odin will help students make sense later of *Paradise Lost* and *Lord of the Rings*—which is not completely wrong. We often speak of lighting fires rather than filling buckets, but we don't want empty buckets either; it's good to recognize names, so that we don't end up like that Agatha Christie villain who got caught because she mixed up Paris in France with Paris of Troy. It's not a bad thing to know things.

But if we are really searching out the reasons that Charlotte Mason plunked down that comment about *Tanglewood Tales* in the middle of a chapter about the planting of ideas and the growth of knowledge, then we have to look deeper. In *Formation of Character*, Mason writes something important:

> It is well we should…recognise, once for all, that personal culture is hardly a legitimate aim. [But] we are allowed to seek knowledge for the sake of knowledge, culture of body and mind for the sake of serviceableness; and, recognising this, we give our lives an impersonal aspect. We look at pictures and read books for the sake of the pictures and the books, and not at all for our sakes. Our children carry forward this larger view of life. They feel, think, and labour without sparing as occasion calls upon them; they live, that is, the common life, and are not stranded in an inlet of individual culture. (p. 302)

Reading literature, in other words, isn't something we do for our own benefit; any more than nature study or picture study or music appreciation is all about our individual likes and dislikes. Literature isn't to be read because it's fun. It isn't even just to give us information. It's to give us a larger view of life, to rescue us from our "inlets of individual culture" and to give us hearts for service, of God and other people. In *Ten Ways to Destroy the Imagination of Your Child*, Anthony Esolen says that if we want to kill imagination, we should "mire the child in the inanities of his own time and place." But our aim is to *release* children, and adults, from the inanities, the boredom, the loneliness, of this time and place. These oldest of stories are the "common property" of all humans, and their special power is that they take us *out* of ourselves, show us something *bigger* and *other* than ourselves.

In Hawthorne's story "The Chimaera," several young children, along with their sarcastic teenage sister Primrose, are listening to their friend Eustace Bright tell them the story of the winged horse Pegasus. When they get to the final scene, where Bellerophon "slipped off the enchanted bridle from the head of the marvelous steed" and offered Pegasus his freedom, Hawthorne says:

> All their eyes were dancing in their heads, except those of Primrose. In her eyes there were positively tears; for she was conscious of something in the legend which the rest of them were not yet old enough to feel. Child's story as it was, the student had contrived to breathe through it the ardor, the generous hope, and the imaginative enterprise of youth.
>
> "I forgive you, now, Primrose," said [Eustace], "for all your ridicule of myself and my stories. One tear pays for a great deal of laughter."

Even the usually mocking Primrose is lifted, if only briefly, out of her "inlet of individual culture," and sees her place in the "common life" through such an unexpected means as the story of a flying horse. We want our children to "carry forward this larger view of life," which is why we're opening the storehouse. It's not an object lesson, not scripted or programmed; it's just what can happen, what does happen.

Sprayed By Painted Ships

> [There's a] story that's told so often, of how man once lived in a golden age or a garden of Eden or the Hesperides, or a happy island kingdom in the Atlantic, how that world was lost, and how we some day may be able to get it back again... (Northrop Frye, *The Educated Imagination*)

Earlier in *Parents and Children* (p. 47), Mason writes that "fairy-tales are so dear to children because their spirits fret against the hard and narrow limitations of time and place and substance; they cannot breathe freely in a material world." Through nature walks and other explorations, they begin to learn that the universe is an amazing place, it is even bigger and stranger than they first thought. And, like a second character named Eustace, they will have to come to terms with another reality even beyond that everyday world, wonderful as it is; one which allows painted ships to spray salt water through picture frames and which might pull them into the story as well.

In *The Voyage of the Dawn Treader*, C. S. Lewis sums up Eustace Scrubb's educational deficit (we won't even get into his character issues) by saying that he had read none of the right books. Partway through the novel, after being accidentally carried into Narnia by that same ship, Eustace finds himself alone in a dragon's cave. He has no idea what to do in this situation, because the books he has read "had a lot to say about exports and imports and governments and drains, but … were weak on dragons." He discovers piles of gold and jewels in the cave, and his first thought is that he could sell it and make lots of money, because Narnia doesn't have income tax. Unfortunately, he then falls asleep "on a dragon's hoard with greedy, dragonish thoughts in his heart," and turns into a dragon himself.

That's the point where reading fairy tales and mythology makes some people very nervous. Mason has been encouraging us to open the door to the storehouse of ideas and let children wander around inside it; but what if this storeroom or cave turns out to be spiritually dangerous? What if our children get so hooked on these stories that they turn into dragons? Or get mixed up about God and the gods? We might assume that these concerns come from the parents and teachers, that the children have fewer hangups about these things than we do. But sometimes it's the other way around, and the questions and objections are raised by children themselves, which leaves their parents wondering if they are doing something wrong by leading them into these unsafe or uncomfortable places. These are not concerns to be laughed at, especially when they come from children's sensitive hearts. But may I offer a few thoughts on this?

First, Lewis says that Eustace's trouble in the dragon's cave came about because he was under-educated and under-equipped. To quote something we've been hearing often over the past few years, too many of us are living in a "disenchanted" world. This is why Jason Baxter wrote a whole book called *The Medieval Mind of C. S. Lewis*, trying to point out that contemporary ways of thinking, knowing, and believing are not necessarily better or truer than old ways. The medieval mindset allowed people to live in this world but also to believe that there was more going on outside of the everyday things—or, that those other things were also a part of the everyday, like goblins living under the castle. We post-moderns put tight parameters around what we believe is real, and the separation and disconnect between the natural world and anything beyond it are now, too often, the norm. Like Eustace, we have the facts, but we're missing the meaning, and that may leave us unprepared when we face our own goblins and dragons.

Second, those who object to "doing mythology" in the early years often misunderstand what kind of stories are being read, or how they are to be presented. Louis Markos, in *The Myth Made Fact: Reading Greek and Roman Mythology Through Christian Eyes,* says that "[myths] need to be told, lovingly and dramatically, in such a way as to engage the full person: mind, heart, soul, and imagination." Those are exactly the sorts of books that the PNEU recommended, and that's the way they should be read. For example, *A Wonder Book* and *Tanglewood Tales* do not give many details about the lives of the gods. Most of the stories are about humans in a world where greedy sailors are changed into pigs, young men ride flying horses, and kind-hearted old people are given a magic milk pitcher that never runs dry. The next mythology book we read in AO, Charles Kingsley's *The Heroes*, contains only three stories about the Greek superheroes Perseus, Jason, and Theseus. If you want more of a catalogue-type book, that would be the d'Aulaires' *Book of Greek Myths*, which is popular with children who enjoy many details, but for others it can be like drinking from a firehose; and it seems to me that reading it too soon gives children a very different experience from the one Mason envisioned. She didn't open the mythology storehouse by listing which god was responsible for thunder or war or healing, or who was whose mother or sister or daughter, but rather by taking the soft-pedaling approach of Hawthorne, who, I think, caught more of the human spirit.

I experienced something of that myself recently, when I was working through the retelling of Norse myths called *The Heroes of Asgard*. When I started reading it, I expected sea battles and Viking raids. But the Norse stories are about a large family of gods who fall in love and get married, help each other out of jams, drink (lots of) mead, write poetry, and make shady deals to get sparkly jewelry. These gods can also be killed, in battles or even with an uncooperative piece of mistletoe; and when they grieve, they expect the whole world to grieve along with them.

The character that I identified with most was a goddess named Iduna. Iduna is married to Bragi, the god of poetry, which is a job that keeps him very busy, but Iduna doesn't mind because she has her own very important job, growing apples. She can't leave the boundaries of the orchard, but that's fine with her because she's so busy keeping everyone supplied with apples, and it's her joy to do this, since her apples are a sort of superfood that keeps all the gods young and healthy. One day the untrustworthy god Loki tricks Iduna into leaving the orchard, by telling her that there is another apple grower who might be giving her competition. Iduna falls for this, and as soon as she steps through the gate, she is kidnapped by an enemy; it turns out that Loki was just using her to pay off a debt. So Iduna disappears without a trace, and without her and the apples, all the other gods start to get wrinkled and droopy, kind of like a *Star Trek* episode where people turn a hundred years old in ten minutes. There is even a sort of angel of death who shows up at the Asgard dinner table, apparently waiting for the main course. Even Loki is shocked at how much damage he's done, so he finally admits that he might know where Iduna might be, and (spoiler alert) she is rescued and the apples are restored, and the angel of death stomps off back to the underworld, still hungry.

Many women reading this can relate to Iduna; many of us are apple-growers of one sort or another. As we read this, we might think about the ways that God uses our talents to bless those around us. We might also notice that false ideas can sneak in and make us compare our work with that of others, even luring us away from the orchard. Iduna, to me, seems less like a deity and more like a human woman who rejoices and worries and nourishes her family. Her hope that breaking the rules, just once, won't matter causes her not only to be taken away from the garden, but brings grief and death to the others as well, until she is finally found and brought home. If Primrose could shed tears over Bellerophon and Pegasus, we can feel justified in remembering Iduna when we cut up a plate of apples.

Something Real and Other

Now, I do want to make it clear that by saying that while it's valuable to find your own meaning in a story, that doesn't mean you see yourself and only yourself there. We can value a painting or a story

Each Tells Its Own Tale

for the ways it allows us to experience joy or sadness; and for the connection it can give us with others who have come before, in the same way that cards in library books used to show the names of all the earlier borrowers. We keep going back to a poem or a piece of music not because we can totally make sense of it, but for the ways that it points us to God and allows us to experience something of His glory. That doesn't always line up with the current understanding of relating a text only to the reader's own experience, in the same way that the practice of narration doesn't line up with the goal of self-expression. But in the same way that narration allows an individual mind to take hold of the story, the practice of valuing it for its own truth and beauty, and for the beauty it can bring to the world, allows the mind—or the heart—to make it its own, in an even better and truer way.

Let's go back to that place in *Parents and Children* where Mason writes, "...let words convey ideas as he is able to bear them. Buttercup, primrose, dandelion, magpie, each tells its own tale..." There is, perhaps, an extra reason why the passage about nature study comes before the one about *Tanglewood* and Plutarch's *Lives*. In the beginning stages, when we're very young, we need to see and name, to observe and pay attention to the things around us. We need to do all this before we can transfer that mental picture-making skill to imaginative literature, including fairy tales and mythology (which might be one argument for using only lightly-illustrated books). Anthony Esolen says, "People whose eyes cannot rest on something as beautiful as a stretch of sea and sky can hardly be expected to dwell upon an imaginary sea or an imaginary sky" (p. 207). I think one of the key words there is "rest"; Esolen asks us to "rest our eyes," not meaning close them or relax them, but fix them, keep them looking, using that other meaning of "rest," the one that is like the French word *rester*, to stay (kind of like "park it there"). Esolen uses the word "dwell"; but we can't even think about "dwelling" if we're not ready for "resting." We need to practice "resting" our minds and our eyes on our physical surroundings before we can apply that skill to something we see in a painting, or, even more challenging, to something we hear about in words, and then use our own minds to translate it into a visual image.

Resting, in that sense, means paying attention.

To Charlotte Mason educators, attention is a familiar topic; but when we talk about developing the habit of attention in our children, we, again, often stick to the practical side. We focus on how it will help them listen to lessons and then narrate, or maybe how it will help them to be useful in taking accurate messages to a neighbour. All that is good! But learning to pay attention goes much deeper than that. British psychiatrist Iain McGilchrist published a book in 2021 titled *The Matter with Things: Our Brains, Our Delusions and the Unmaking of the World*. In it he writes, "What is required is an attentive response to something real and other than ourselves." He also says, "Attention changes the world. How you attend to it changes what it is you find there. What you find then governs the kind of attention you will think it appropriate to pay in the future." This is what Mason has been talking about all along: the finding or hearing or seeing of something "real and other than ourselves" that pulls us to full attention, that makes us question, brings us joy, teaches us reverence, and allows us to carry forward that larger view of life.

We can now go back to that poem of Mary Oliver's:

> I don't know exactly what a prayer is.
>
> I do know how to pay attention, how to fall down
>
> Into the grass, how to kneel down in the grass,
>
> How to be idle and blessed, how to stroll through the fields,
>
> Which is what I have been doing all day.

The ability to attend is what allows us to experience the "science of relations"; to not only see the author's signature Sharpied throughout the world, but to allow Him to speak to us and teach us. If we hear and see that, we also begin to make connections with the world of ideas; "the best thoughts, stored up in books."

Pools of Reality

Another reason that parent-educators might want to reconsider their hesitancy about reading mythology is its relation to the classical tradition. In his book *The Myth Made Fact*, Louis Markos says that "the great myths both spark our imagination and instill in us a desire to seek out virtue and avoid vice." These stories reach into places deep inside us that more recent or realistic stories do not, like King Midas asking how you can possibly have too much gold; or the old couple who ask to spend eternity together, and receive their wish; or the various myths where people are told not to open something or peek at someone, but they give in to their curiosity and spoil everything. There are certainly some children or situations where discernment says that it would be better to wait a bit, or even quite a long while; but those would seem to be exceptional cases. Most children will not turn into dragons by being given permission to explore the cave, and, in fact, that early allowance of imagination is what may keep them safe when they do so.

As a final response to why we need myths, let's look at another Narnia book, *The Magician's Nephew*. Wicked Uncle Andrew has used a magic ring to send Digory's friend Polly, along with a guinea pig, to someplace unknown; and Digory agrees to put on another magic ring to go there and bring them back. He finds Polly and the guinea pig in a magic wood surrounded by pools of water, each of which, they discover, could take them to a different world, including one that goes back to their own. As Polly and Digory aren't in any hurry to get back, especially to see any more of Uncle Andrew, they decide to dive into an unknown pool, which begins a whole new adventure. "The Wood Between the Worlds," as they discover, is "a place that isn't any of the worlds, but once you've found that place you can get into them all."

I think when we begin to explore the mythology of any culture, it's like diving through one of the pools and coming up in another land that is self-contained and has its own version of reality. It might have fauns and talking beavers, or hobbits and elves, or black cauldrons and truthful harps, or Valhalla and mead horns. Each of these worlds is an imaginary, what-if place, but also a place where hobbits or assistant pig-keepers or talking mice are forced to choose generosity or greed, courage or cowardice. They meet people, sometimes friends, sometimes enemies. They make mistakes, get tricked, forget important things, but they also take risks, make friendships, and search for truth and beauty. As junior explorers in the realm of ideas, our children need both the safe launching place of the wood, and the adventure of the unknown worlds; and, as Polly reminds Digory, it's also a good idea to clearly mark your own pool before you go diving into any others.

And here we can find the last lines of Mary Oliver's poem:

> Tell me, what else should I have done?
>
> Doesn't everything die at last, and too soon?

Borrowed Riches

> Tell me, what is it you plan to do
> With your one wild and precious life?

In *The Myth Made Fact*, Louis Markos refers to C. S. Lewis and his journey of faith. Even before he was a Christian, Lewis was interested in what was called the universal myth of a dying god, and he believed that Jesus could be a Hebrew version of that god. His friend J. R. R. Tolkien suggested to him that maybe it was the other way around, that Christ was the "myth that became fact." Much later, Lewis wrote an essay with that title, "Myth Became Fact," which is where Markos got the title for his own book. In that essay, Lewis wrote, "Myth is not truth but reality (truth is always about something, but reality is that about which truth is)..." Markos adds, "What Lewis helped us to do—indeed, what he gave us permission to do—was to listen for God's voice in a hundred different mediums...And he is often powerfully and intimately present in myths."

To this we might add: to give a child the key to the storehouse is to show them a hundred different magic pools, each one leading to a place where God's voice can be heard, each one an opportunity to look for the author's name Sharpied in the strangest of places. Why should we deny them that wild and precious adventure of life?

I hope that you will find time, yourselves, to be "idle and blessed." Kneel in the grass, or fall into it; stroll through the fields; saunter through the storehouse. And enjoy your explorations.

Still Not Fish: The Epiphany of King Midas

> He took one of the nice little trouts on his plate, and, by way of experiment, touched its tail with his finger. To his horror, it was immediately transmuted from an admirably fried brook-trout into a gold-fish, though not one of those gold-fishes which people often keep in glass globes, as ornaments for the parlor. No; but it was really a metallic fish, and looked as if it had been very cunningly made by the nicest goldsmith in the world. Its little bones were now golden wires; its fins and tail were thin plates of gold; and there were the marks of the fork in it, and all the delicate, frothy appearance of a nicely fried fish, exactly imitated in metal. A very pretty piece of work, as you may suppose; only King Midas, just at that moment, would much rather have had a real trout in his dish than this elaborate and valuable imitation of one. (Nathaniel Hawthorne, "The Golden Touch" in *A Wonder Book*)

We have heard a great deal lately on the topic of imitation (via artificial intelligence) vs. real. AI may create something cunning, delicate, even frothy, with marks of the fork in it; but it's still not fish.

However, for educators, the story of Midas can hold even deeper meaning. Charlotte Mason did not write about serving children metallic fish, but she did mention feasts of "smoke and lukewarm water," or, more literally, "stale commonplaces" (*Philosophy of Education*, p. 44). We might even say that when administrators and curriculum developers touch the king's breakfast with their well-intentioned fingers, they almost invariably turn the food into something glittering but inedible. At the very least, it affects the trout; at the worst (as in the story of Midas and his daughter), it transforms the children themselves.

> It had been a favorite phrase of Midas, whenever he felt particularly fond of the child, to say that she was worth her weight in gold. And now the phrase had become literally true. And now, at last, when it was

> too late, he felt how infinitely a warm and tender
> heart, that loved him, exceeded in value all the
> wealth that could be piled up betwixt the earth and
> sky!

Edith Hamilton, in her *Mythology*, comments that Midas "meant no harm; he merely did not use any intelligence."

What shall we do to repair this damage, to restore life to these warm and tender hearts? In Hawthorne's version, Midas was told to sprinkle river water over the affected objects (and people) in his palace. But the true healing of King Midas began with the recognition that a real trout was even more beautiful than one made of gold. The restoration of education requires that we recognize the value of the "lines of nature," and that we allow Nature and the Holy Spirit their proper "time and scope."

And that can be...an epiphany.

"Even to a Boy": Lessons from Uncle Plutarch

This was written as a sequel to the previous talk on mythology.

We have heard about the steps that children take into the "storehouse of ideas," which was, by and large, Mason's term for literature and history, or what she also called the knowledge of God and man. When children are still at the stage of recognition and naming, they are in the right place to be reading *Tanglewood Tales* and other books of that kind; and when they are a little older, Mason says, we move them up to Plutarch's *Lives*.

She assumes, of course, that that she's not saying anything surprising there, and that we'll all be nodding our heads. Once upon a time, reading Plutarch was something of a norm, at least for the children of educated parents. There's a wonderful quote by the son of the American writer Ralph Waldo Emerson, talking about his father's particular attachment to Plutarch. The younger Emerson writes,

> When I was fourteen years old, he put Plutarch's *Lives* into my hand and bade me read two pages every week-day and ten every holiday. It seemed at first an irksome task, but my mother asked me to read them aloud to her, and this made it easier. Lycurgus's training of the Spartan boys, Archimedes's amazing military engineering in the defence of Syracuse, Hannibal's passage of the Alps, Scipio's magnanimity and Cæsar's courage and genius won their own way, as my father knew they would with a boy, and, what is by no means common with authors, the personality of the writer also, as, for instance, where he drops the narrative to hotly censure the meanness of Cato the Elder in selling his slaves when they were past service. The style of Plutarch could commend itself even to a boy.

But we are in a different century, when it is not only unlikely that a father would expect his son to read two pages of Plutarch a day, and that the boy would read the book out loud to his mother, but even less so that even the parent knows who or what Plutarch is, or why anyone would want to read him. What is it that made Plutarch's *Lives* not only one of the PNEU curriculum standbys, but also one of the most-read books in America up until about the end of the nineteenth century; and what then made it disappear so completely by the time any of us were being given books to read?

Fifty years ago, when I was being trotted around flea markets with my parents on weekend afternoons, it was common to come across old copies of *Black Beauty*, *Little Women*, *Alice in Wonderland*; or sets of classic books which might include oddball titles like *White Fang*. But no twentieth-century children's publisher (that I ever heard of anyway) produced a set with Plutarch's *Lives*, not even in a retelling. And it definitely wasn't on the book-order forms we got at school.

For anyone who doesn't know this yet, Plutarch was a Greek historian and civic leader, who lived towards the end of the first century A.D. and then into the second. He wrote a series of biographies of about forty-eight famous Greeks and Romans, called the *Parallel Lives*, which is usually what we're referring to when we say, "you should read Plutarch." They're called the *Parallel Lives* because Plutarch tried to team up each Greek life with a Roman one. Jumping ahead to the sixteenth century, Thomas North based the first English translation of Plutarch on a French edition rather than the original Greek; but it was a very popular book in England nonetheless, and it gave William Shakespeare source material for plays like *Julius Caesar* and *Coriolanus*. There have been other, more accurate English translations of Plutarch since then; but North's is one that Mason mentions particularly, though she also quotes from a nineteenth century translation called Langhorne's. There are also more recent translations such as those by David Hicks. It's fine to use whatever you have available and are comfortable with, but sometimes you might want to look at something older or newer, just to change things up. And that's all we need to say here about translations.

So, when people say they're reading "Plutarch," they usually mean the *Lives*, but those make up less than half of Plutarch's surviving works. A set of his writings called the *Moralia* are made up of everything else in the world that he found interesting: essays on literature, religious issues, the education of children, something called "Should an Old Man Take Part in Public Life?", and advice to a bride and groom. Plutarch also wrote a collection of dialogues, called *Table Talk*, drawn from conversations from the dinner parties that he hosted as part of his public duties. He liked to tell stories, of course, but he found it just as stimulating to hear what other people had been doing and thinking about, and he entertained all kinds of people, from scholars and civil servants to farmers. Do you remember what Emerson Junior said about his reading of Plutarch? "In what is by no means common with authors, the personality of the writer won its way." He seemed to feel that he had met Plutarch personally, almost as if he had been allowed to sit in at those parties and hear all the interesting talk. In that story Emerson mentions about Cato the Elder, Plutarch is writing about a Roman orator who, he said, "exerted and practiced his eloquence through all the neighbourhood and little villages; thinking it…an all but necessary organ to one who looks forward to something above a mere humble and inactive life." But he might also be describing himself, Plutarch, who also led "something above a mere humble and inactive life" by collecting and writing down the stories of others' lives.

He did that so well that, centuries later, Shakespeare read the *Lives*, and so did Montaigne and Rousseau, Goethe and Beethoven, Abraham Lincoln, and Frankenstein's monster.

He wrote in such a way that Ralph Waldo Emerson, in 1858, gave his son a copy of the *Lives*, likely in Langhorne's translation which had come out in a nice new edition a couple of years before that.

And he wrote in such a way that Charlotte Mason read his *Lives* to her students and told us to go and do likewise. She says, "I think [the *Lives*] stand alone in literature as teaching that a man is part of the State, that his business is to be of service to the State, but that the value of his service depends upon his personal character" (*School Education*, pp. 280–281).

Those are the general arguments for making Plutarch's *Lives* a part of the curriculum. But what we want to find out here is why and how they got slotted into that particular spot, at the doorstep of Mason's "storehouse of ideas."

Acts of Heroism

I think it might be less about the "heroes," and more about

everyday "heroism." Mythology, as has already been said, is full of classical virtues like Justice, Temperance, Prudence, and Courage, and even young children can absorb those ideas from stories like "King Midas" and "Pandora's Box." As they move up to Plutarch's *Lives*, they will see the virtues applied in big ways by rulers and warriors; but the hope is that they will take those same ideas, value them, and find ways to use them in their own everyday lives.

For example, let's talk about the virtue called Fortitude. Mason describes it in *School Education*, saying:

> ...when we think how little power we have to do the tiresome things we set ourselves to do every day, we appreciate the compelling power a child can use, given a strong enough impulse. The long name, Fortitude, would have its effect on the little boy in the dentist's hands...and the girl who finds it a fine thing to endure hardness will not make a fuss about her physical sensations. She will be pained for the want of fortitude which called the reproof, 'Could ye not watch with me one hour?' and will brace herself to bear, that she may be able to serve. (pp. 110–111)

We would all probably agree that Fortitude is a commendable and practical character trait to develop. But please notice the very first thing Mason said in that quote: "...when we think how little power we have to do the tiresome things we set ourselves to do every day..." We are being asked to do not just hard things, but even worse, tiresome things. And not just occasionally, as in great emergencies, but every day. This might explain, as well as any more complicated theory, why Plutarch and Charlotte Mason suddenly became yesterday's teachers. The thinking went from "How can we become brave enough to do the things that might hurt?" to "Why should we have to do things that hurt at all?"

Let's go back to the mid-nineteenth century and Ralph Waldo Emerson. There is a direct connection between his philosophy and that of Louisa May Alcott; Emerson was Alcott's writing mentor and a family friend. So, in Alcott's novels, that theme of Fortitude comes up frequently, of doing small things faithfully, especially tiresome things that nobody thanks you for. In the first chapter of *Little Women*, set during the U. S. Civil War, the March sisters get a letter from their father, who is a chaplain in the army, saying that he hopes "that they will be loving children to [their mother], will do their duty faithfully, fight their bosom enemies bravely, and conquer themselves so beautifully that when I come back to them I may be fonder and prouder than ever of my little women." The girls immediately make resolutions to be less selfish and vain, especially the main character Jo, who feels that "keeping her temper at home [is] a much harder task than facing a rebel or two down South." But that kind of resolution is now viewed as nostalgia, very sweet but not required for our own time. Even in Emerson's day, individualism and materialism were competing for space with older ideas of loyalty and service; and characters like Alcott's were not always in the mainstream; in fact, that's the theme of her novel *An Old-Fashioned Girl*.

And then we get into the twentieth century and progressive education. Many of you will have read Dorothy Canfield Fisher's children's novel *Understood Betsy*. Well-meaning but anxious Aunt Frances is raising little Elizabeth Ann according to the latest child psychology books–but it's not going well. Later, when Elizabeth Ann is sent to live with other relatives in Vermont, she sees her Great-Aunt Abigail "reading out of a small, worn old book. Elizabeth Ann could see its title, *Essays of Emerson* [yes, that Emerson]. A book with that name had always laid on the center table [at home], but that copy was all new and shiny, and Elizabeth Ann had never seen anybody look inside it."

It's never mentioned again, but that book sitting on Aunt Abigail's nightstand, and the fact that it's a worn old copy instead of just a "new and shiny" one, tells us a whole lot of things. If Elizabeth Ann had looked inside it, she would have seen titles like "Self Reliance," "Heroism," "Nature," and "Prudence." And those titles describe what our main character becomes, as she grows from fearful Elizabeth Ann into resourceful and generous Betsy. The fact that *Understood Betsy* was published in 1917, and that its author mentions Aunt Frances taking "a correspondence course in mothercraft from a school in Chicago which teaches that business by mail," also matches the point at which we started to lose it, Emerson and Plutarch-wise.

There are certain thinkers who view what we're lacking in today's world not just from an Emersonian moral angle, but from a more spiritual or supernatural one. In his biography of C. S. Lewis, *The Narnian*, Alan Jacobs states that Lewis's mind was "characterized by...omnivorous attentiveness," and especially *"a willingness to be enchanted"* (p. xxi, italics his). Can we stop right there and ponder that? We move from attentiveness (and not just any attentiveness, but "omnivorous attentiveness") to enchantment, and back again. We go from Mary Oliver's poem "The Summer Day"; through a teenage girl shedding tears over a moment of love (granted, it's a horse story); to the Roman consul Brutus making the hardest decision of his life; to the story of the Gospel; and then back again to watching grasshoppers. One of the pastors at the church I attend is known for his referring, in every other sermon, to the first chapters of Genesis; and with that I think Oliver's question "Who made the world?" would agree. But if we don't ask these questions, if we don't have attention, if we don't look for enchantment, then we are shut in, stunted, and fearful, like Mary and Colin before they discover *The Secret Garden.*

Rod Dreher also describes our contemporary world as one that has lost its sense of enchantment and wonder.

> ...the vivid sense of spiritual reality that our enchanted ancestors had has been drained of its life force...without the living experience of enchantment present and accessible, and at the pulsating center of life in Christ, the faith loses its wonder. And when it loses its wonder, it loses its power to console us, change us, and call us to acts of heroism.
> (*Living in Wonder*, p. 9)

But let's reverse that idea and say that a faith filled with a vivid, living, very present sense of spiritual reality *does* have the power to console us, change us, and call us to acts of heroism.

And that is, by and large, why we're reading Plutarch.

Making This Work

Even if we're convinced that reading Plutarch is worthwhile, we may still have questions about how to manage that difficult reading. It's unlikely that our children are going to be like Emerson Junior, willing to simply take the book and read it out loud. Also, there are bits of Plutarch that aren't good for young ones to hear. So, we read it to them as long as necessary; but, as in a nature walk, we will allow the children to be the lookers and listeners. We accept that much of it will go by them in that first pass, but that the important ideas will nevertheless catch hold and sprout.

Mason uses an interesting word to describe the handing over of the storehouse keys: "leaving the child's mind to deal with the *matter* as it can." Not just "the topic", or "the subject," but Matter—that physical substance that Mason later says, "becomes a part of us just as literally as was yesterday's dinner."

> ...we visualise the scene, are convinced by the arguments, take pleasure in the turn of the sentences and frame our own upon them; in that particular passage or chapter has been received into us and become a part of us just as literally as was yesterday's dinner; nay, more so, for yesterday's dinner is of little account tomorrow; but several months, perhaps hence, we shall be able to narrate the passage we had, so to say, consumed and grown upon with all the vividness, detail and accuracy of the first telling. (*Philosophy of Education*, pp. 173–174)

To paraphrase Mason, it must have been something we ate.

But we're back to the question of "how": how do we keep from getting in the way, but still give the necessary support and encouragement for these difficult books? Here's Mason's advice, again from *Philosophy of Education*, and it's rather blunt:

> "...we may not ask questions to help the child to reason, paint fancy pictures to help him to imagine, draw out moral lessons to quicken his conscience. These things take place as involuntarily as processes of digestion." (pp. 173–174)

We may feel a bit over our heads with the instruction that teachers should write the names of important people and places on the blackboard, as a reference for the students. That assumes that we already know which of those names matter; well, sometimes we do, and sometimes we don't, which is why I've spent all these years writing Plutarch study guides. Mason's general point of view is that study guides are a waste of time, mostly because she wants students to think and discover for themselves as much as possible, rather than having everything handed to them. She does recommend with Plutarch, though, that students refer to a classical dictionary; and the student editions that the PNEU used (back in the day) included at least a few notes in the back; so it wasn't entirely sink or swim for them. I justify my own efforts by saying that it's not so much the students who need that extra bit of help and boost of confidence these days, as their parents and teachers; but my real aim in writing the study guides is to work myself out of a job. Think about this: this next generation, those who have grown up thinking of Plutarch's *Lives* as familiar to them as yesterday's dinner, won't hesitate to open up a full Dryden's or even a North's translation with their own children. And that's as it should be.

Picture It

But since we're not all completely fluent in Plutarch yet, it seems there's room for a little practical help in how to teach it. The first, and really the only truly important rule about reading the *Lives* in a Charlotte Mason setting, is that students read the text *once*, or have it read to them; and then they narrate it in some form. *Philosophy of Education* offers us a mini teacher's guide:

> Trusting to mind memory we visualise the scene, are convinced by the arguments, take pleasure in the turn of the sentences and frame our own upon them...several months, perhaps hence, we shall be able to narrate the passage we had, so to say, consumed and grown upon with all the vividness, detail and accuracy of the first telling. (pp. 173–174)

To use Mason's dinner metaphor in a very careful sense, we can't eat the same meal twice; or at least, it won't make the same impression on us. That doesn't mean we can't eat pepperoni pizza a hundred times; but when we're focusing on the impact of *ideas* from one of these key books, the power of a fresh hearing is something we don't want to waste.

One of the PNEU teachers, who signed her work as "Miss Ambler," said this in *The Parents' Review*:

> If we want to offer ideas by the means of early history in the form of biography, we come at once to Plutarch, the prince of biographers. We take the children straight to the fountain-head and introduce them to this dear deliberate old gentleman, who will, in a leisurely way, tell them

Lessons from Uncle Plutarch

delightfully graphic stories in simple language and who will not omit a single detail, so that even the child can think of no more questions to ask.

Another teacher, "Miss Parish," said:

We do not *tell* the tales, we know we cannot, we *read* them as well as we know how and without comment, unless questions are asked. (italics mine)

The key, according to these teachers, and Mason herself, is encouraging students to create what they call a "mental word-picture." It goes back to that passage in *Parents and Children* about the child taking a walk, seeing all kinds of things outside, asking for the names of things, coming home and talking about it, and still being able to visualize what he saw, without turning it into one of those objectionable object lessons. One way for teachers to help is to build on whatever students already know; maybe there's a familiar character, a place they have already read about. Another idea is that, like the nature walk, you can ask the children to listen for something, such as a repeated name or word. Like nature walks, it's best not to overdo this, especially at the beginning; you head for home before everyone's grumpy and complaining.

Here's one more suggestion, which comes from a description of Bible lessons in the primary grades. Mason says, "Before the close of the lesson, the teacher brings out such new thoughts of God or new points of behaviour as the reading has afforded…" (*Philosophy of Education*, p. 163). Now, that doesn't mean we say, "Look how Demosthenes stuck to his training plan to be a great orator, how he stayed in his little study room for days at a time and didn't even think about going out for fun—ahem, have you finished your math page?" But we do want children to notice, somehow, that the story reveals something about character; that the choices people make do matter, to themselves and to others. How can we do that?

One way is to, occasionally, give your own narration after the students are done, not to try to do it better than they did, but to emphasize one key scene that you hope they will remember. In the old sitcom *The Golden Girls,* the elderly mother, Sophia, tells stories that always start something like this, "Picture it. Sicily, 1922." Well, you don't have to say, "Picture it," but that's what you're doing. This kind of wrapping-up is not at all forbidden in C.M., though perhaps it is a tool we haven't used enough; and since Plutarch is often going to be one of the subjects that is read aloud together, it's the perfect opportunity for us to do that little bit extra. We are not "telling" the students what to think about the story; we are simply "showing." Miss Ambler warns, "The words, however, must only be very few, and used more to direct the working out of the train of thought in the child's mind, and must therefore depend upon the child and the point of view he takes."

I think she has already told us how to do that, by calling Plutarch "this dear deliberate old gentleman." Picture it. Chaeronea. 120 A.D. Imagine that Plutarch comes to your house, and the kids gather around to hear his stories. They call him Professor Plutarch, Uncle Plutarch, even Grandpa Plutarch, whatever; but he begins to talk, and they listen. Maybe he rambles and loses his train of thought. Occasionally you have to put your hands over a sensitive child's ears; or take one of them outside if the story gets a bit too violent. But you don't interrupt, right? You just let Plutarch tell the story. And that is, more or less, what we need to do as teachers: stay in the room, be aware of what's going on, but let the storytelling come from the master. Afterwards, the children narrate, and then you can do your "picture it" too. Maybe there's something to add to a timeline or a Book of Centuries, or something to look up on a map.

Now I do need to point out that sometimes when listeners don't ask enough questions, they can miss important things. The things they ask about may not have occurred to us, or they might not be the things we think are important. For instance, children listening to *Understood Betsy* might not have any interest in that Emerson book of Aunt Abigail's, but they might ask about other things in the story that do puzzle them, like what the "cars" are that the girls need to find enough money to ride home on. (They might also want to make applesauce and maple syrup candy.) But you hope they *will* ask questions, unlike Elizabeth Ann who has never wondered much about what's going on or how things work. Like her, children might need help to learn to ask things like how and where. In our desire to stand back and let the book speak, our mistake may be forgetting that we can't just walk out the door and see its context; we might have to create it in the minds of the listeners. Just as we want to study trilliums growing in the woods and willows by a stream, Plutarch's *Lives* make more sense when we support the ideas with the necessary history and geography. Plutarch-reading students are at a good age to be working with maps; but the story itself should be what brings the map to life, not the other way around.

Also, a bit of cultural information can be helpful, especially when you're starting a new *Life* with unfamiliar characters. You know your students best; maybe they're all about the clothing, or maybe it's the weapons, or the food in the story that gets them paying attention, that helps them start seeing a clearer picture of what's going on. Simply reading the *Lives* is adequate, if it's absolutely all you can manage; but it seems like a waste to miss out completely on where and when they happened.

Finally, there's the problem of mature content. Having heard so much about reading Plutarch with children, we may forget that they were not his original intended audience. If you want to use the already-onced-over AO versions, they are free to use on the website; or if you prefer to do your own on-the-fly editing, any standard translation into your own language will do. Exercise a mite more caution with contemporary translations, though, as they can sometimes make things a little *too* clear for young listeners.

Such Portions and Such Quantities

Let's talk a little more about what we find in Plutarch, and why Charlotte Mason tagged him so conspicuously near the storehouse doorway. Imagine that we're venturing in there, making discoveries, and one of the first and greatest things we uncover is Valour. This can be called Courage or Bravery, but it also has anatomical synonyms like Backbone and Guts—which brings us back to Fortitude. Plutarch's *Lives* are full of Valour and Fortitude: not only sword-wielding valour that wins battles, but integrity-valour, intolerance-of-corrupt-bullying-power valour, persistence-without-pampering valour, and fight-the-good-fight valour. In all those modes, valour is heroism.

In *Ten Ways to Destroy the Imagination of Your Child*, Anthony Esolen says, "The hero stretches our imagination. He introduces us, for better or for worse, to possibilities we had never considered. He extends the limits of what is human. If he does so in the service of something good and noble, we love him so much the better for it" (p. 143). Whenever we meet heroes in literature, whether they're aiming peashooters at trucks, carrying magic rings up mountains, or defending the bridge over the Tiber River, we see something of what we could be, what we could do. I mentioned earlier that scene in Louisa May Alcott's *Little Women*, where the March sisters receive a letter from their father, and how each one then decides to practice valour until he comes home from the war, just by doing the things that she personally finds hardest. I think that the letter strikes an extra chord in the daughters' hearts because they know their father is living among courageous young soldiers, and they want to live up to that heroic ideal as well.

And how do we bring children to this place of extended imagination, can-you-picture-it, and could-we-do-it?

> We are careful not to dilute life for them, but to present such portions to them in such quantities as they can readily receive...[we] do not take too much upon ourselves, but leave time and scope for the workings of Nature and of a higher Power than Nature herself. (*Parents and Children*, p. 232)

This is what we do: we open the storehouse of enchantment and ideas. We start out simply with mythology, then stretch the heroic imagination with Plutarch. We do not dilute, we do not take too much upon ourselves, we leave time and scope for the Holy Spirit to do its work in our children's minds.

And if anyone thinks we're creating prigs, or children who are too lofty-minded to be of any good in this world, I would refer them again to Anthony Esolen, who says that "A hero, even a fictional creation, is like a pack of dynamite, ready to blow any mountain of heaped-up conformity and dullness sky high" (*Ten Ways*, p. 146).

Endings, Beginnings, and T. S. Eliot

This was a talk given at the Deep in the Heart of AO conference in 2016. It has been edited slightly for this book.

In southwestern England, in the county of Somerset, about an hour's drive from Bath, there is a village of 1600 people called East Coker. There's also North Coker, and West Coker, and the villages are connected by deep lanes cut between hills, so if you're walking and a truck comes along, you have to flatten yourself against a wall or a hedgerow until it passes.

On a summer afternoon in 1937, the poet, publisher, editor and critic Thomas Stearns Eliot made a visit to East Coker, because it was the village from which his ancestor Andrew Elyot had left for America. Later, when he was writing the poem by that name which became part of his *Four Quartets*, he drew on his memories of that visit, and one of the first images he included was that approach to the village:

> Now the light falls
> Across the open field, leaving the deep lane
> Shuttered with branches, dark in the afternoon,
> Where you lean against a bank while a van passes,
> And the deep lane insists on the direction
> Into the village...

Recently a journalist, Anthony Gardner, wrote an article on East Coker, and he said the delivery truck drivers still drive through the lanes like maniacs, and there are now factories and new housing around the edges of town. However, he said, the center of the village itself is still very picturesque, full of thatched cottages with rose gardens.

That makes me think of the AmblesideOnline community. In the welcome letter included in the conference booklets, Lynn Bruce wrote, "Even though AmblesideOnline seems bigger than we are these days, it remains a grassroots effort at heart." We began with a small website and an e-group, and then we added another e-group called AmbleRamble to handle more casual conversations. When the load of past and present emails still became too unwieldy, we switched to a forum [and, later, added other social media platforms]. We began with a six-year curriculum; now it's twelve years, or more if you count Year Zero and the in-betweens.

We began with the intention of both protecting our Charlotte Mason curriculum-child and keeping it free for use. The heart of AmblesideOnline is still a vision of education that is an atmosphere, a discipline, and a life, accessible no matter where you live or what your circumstances; and that has *not* changed.

In East Coker, there is also a thirteenth century church called The Church of St. Michael and All Angels. The outside looks a bit like the drawings of Lord's Chapel in Jan Karon's *Mitford* novels. The journalist Anthony Gardner said,

> It is when you stand outside the church door and look back towards the village that you most clearly understand why Eliot loved this place. The grass around the lichen-covered tombs and leaning tombstones is thick with buttercups and daisies; butterflies flit between them, and the ground slopes away to offer an Arcadian view of trees and meadows and distant blue hills.

Eliot was so impressed by this place that, when he died twenty-five years later, he requested that his ashes be buried under the church floor. There is a stone plaque to mark that place, which I'll get to in a minute, and a photograph of Eliot on a column. But Anthony Gardner noticed something else interesting about the church. He said:

> Closer examination of St. Michael's reveals a number of things that do not quite fit. The arches on the north side are not altogether straight; the stained-glass window behind the altar is just off centre; the tower, contrary to usual practice, is built at the east end of the church. Even at its best, it seems, humanity—as Eliot suggests in his poem—is an imperfect part of God's greater pattern.

This is also a good description of the AmblesideOnline community. We are a collection of imperfect, sometimes even *strange* people, from different places, different backgrounds. Our personal lives and circumstances are often far from some imagined ideal. T.S. Eliot wrote in "East Coker" that our knowledge and experience impose a pattern, but that the pattern is "new in every moment, and every moment is a

Endings, Beginnings, and T. S. Eliot

new and shocking valuation of all we have been." For some of us, the patterns we thought we had built up in our own lives have shifted in directions we did not choose, perhaps like the arches and window in St. Michael's Church. We have also seen shifts and changes, sometimes unexpected ones, in the direction and makeup of AO itself. But in the next stanza of the poem, Eliot reminds us that *"The only wisdom we can hope to acquire / Is the wisdom of humility: humility is endless."*

But back to the memorial plaque. Along with Eliot's name and the dates of his birth, 1888, and death, 1965, it quotes the opening and closing sentences of "East Coker":

In my beginning is my end.

In my end is my beginning.

So, beginnings and ends, ends and beginnings. Studies show that going through a doorway seems to affect our memories. It's not just a problem of aging, forgetting what you came for when you go into another room; it has something to do with moving from one place to another. Changes and interruptions make us lose our context, forget where we were and what we wanted, and we struggle to find those places again. The end of Andrew Elyot's life in England was a new page of his family story in America; and Thomas Stearns Eliot must have thought it appropriate that the end of his own earthly life would be in the same place. He said about his poetry, "It wouldn't be what it is if I'd been born in England, and it wouldn't be what it is if I'd stayed in America."

Prufrock

The theme of endings, beginnings, and time in general is explored all the way through *Four Quartets*, and in fact through Eliot's other poetry as well, including his earlier poem "The Love Song of J. Alfred Prufrock." Prufrock is a middle-aged man who feels he is wasting too much time. He wants to do or be something significant, or at least be understood by his friends, especially women, when he tries to talk to them about important things, without them thinking that he's insane or just boring. But he knows he's never going to stand out; he says that if life is a play, he's not Prince Hamlet, but maybe one of the lords like Polonius, "glad to be of use." He also feels "a bit obtuse; At times, indeed, almost ridiculous—Almost, at times, the Fool." When he asks, "Do I dare to eat a peach?", I always thought that was because peaches are messy, but I've also read that his anxiety was that peaches have hard pits, and that he may have been getting loose teeth as he got older, so he didn't want to bite down too hard and break a tooth.

The saddest part of Prufrock is that, in the end, he decides not to take the risks of blurting out his thoughts, of wearing his hair a different way, or of chomping on peaches. He says he has heard the mermaids singing, but that he doesn't believe they are singing to him. Russell Kirk, in his book on Eliot, says that Prufrock, "being infirm of will, creeps back into the prison of Time...The mermaids of the moral imagination will not sing to him." The end of the poem is like the way we sometimes cover ourselves, after we feel we've said too much or spoken too forcefully, by saying, "I'll just go back in my little corner now." It can be hard to risk coming out of that corner; to risk being misunderstood, or looking foolish. But the only real mistake is *not* risking it, because we think it's too weird, or too late, or too dangerous, to bite in.

The Waste Land

Recently I was reading in Second Chronicles where King Solomon prayed in front of the people during the dedication of the new temple. He listed things that might happen where they would need to come together and pray, in times of war or drought and so on. He said:

> If there be dearth in the land, if there be pestilence...
>
> Then what prayer or what supplication soever shall be made of any man, or of all thy people Israel, when every one shall know his own sore and his own grief, and shall spread forth his hands in this house:
>
> Then hear thou from heaven thy dwelling place, and forgive, and render unto every man according unto all his ways, whose heart thou knowest; (for thou only knowest the hearts of the children of men)...
>
> (2 Chronicles 6:28-30)

Solomon recognized that there were not just community problems and sorrows, but that each person had his own needs, and that maybe all that someone experiencing heartbreak or pain could do, was to stretch out his hands towards the temple. He believed that the Lord knew their hearts, that he cared, that he would be merciful. But he also saw that there was *going* to be sorrow, that there *would* be famines and sicknesses and sin. Remember Charlotte Mason's story about the little girl who saw the beggar and came home in tears? Eliot agrees that it is better to have tears than to ignore the pain or not to care, but he also emphasizes the need for moral action. We can't just *feel* sad about things; we also need to *act* in compassion, even if that is only to stretch out our hands alongside someone else's.

Much of Eliot's poetry from the 1920's, especially "The Waste Land" and "The Hollow Men," focuses on the dark side of life: loneliness, sleepless nights, rotten teeth, futility. "The Waste Land" is, on one level, about Europe between the world wars, but it's also about spiritual and moral drought. Even the spring weather is deceptive (and I do know something about that; we had snow halfway through April this year). In the poem, the "Seeker" travels through a forsaken desert, and finally arrives at the Chapel Perilous, a mystical place rooted in the legend of the Fisher King, where those souls brave enough to enter may ask the great questions of life. The Seeker hears the voice of thunder, and the rolling of the thunder resembles the Sanskrit words for "give, sympathize, control." It is a call for less ego, more compassion; a call to self-discipline, will, and action; kind of a Sanskrit "I am, I can, I ought, I will." The Seeker then decides to put his own lands in order, although the world is still a mad place. It's not a final answer, but it's better than just drifting.

Significant Soil

After Eliot's conversion to Anglicanism, when he was about forty, he didn't suddenly start writing happy poems. But he also saw people as part of a larger, longer story, drawing from the past but also contributing something to life in the future. In *Four Quartets*, he wrote,

> We, content at the last
>
> If our temporal reversion nourish
>
> (Not too far from the yew-tree)

The life of significant soil.

If you take what he said there literally, it's what Robin Williams said in *Dead Poets' Society*: we are all, eventually, worm food. But I would like to suggest that nourishing the soil is something that can happen *during* our lives here on earth as well. T.S. Eliot was not just a poet; he was very much engaged with the political and philosophical thought of his time. He edited a quarterly journal called *The Criterion* for about sixteen years, which George Orwell called "possibly the best literary paper we have ever had." When he described himself as a classicist, a small-c conservative, and an Anglo-Catholic, he meant almost the same thing by each of those terms: that his life was not a monologue, like Prufrock's poem, spoken to an empty theater; but rather that he claimed his place in the chain of western culture and in the tradition of Christian worldview and practice. Like the turtle in Holling's *Minn of the Mississippi*, we are, so to speak, paddling down the river with markers of past civilizations buried in the mud beneath us; and the challenge is not only to notice and try to make sense of those artifacts, but to realize that we are swimming in the same river, that it is also our story.

Maybe it is not so impossible to enable others to catch falling stars, to hear mermaids singing, to keep off envy's stinging, and to find honest minds. The homes and classrooms that we create, the beauty that we cultivate, the relationships that we nurture, the belief that education is an atmosphere, a discipline, a life; the value of habit; faithfulness in small things, and perseverance through hard times—all those things will nourish the soil of other lives around us.

Four Quartets

Four Quartets was not the last thing Eliot ever wrote, but it was his last major poem. It began as a series of separate poems, including "East Coker," but it was eventually published as a complete work in 1943. Helen Gardner's book *The Art of T.S. Eliot* explores the poem in depth and makes the point that, unlike some of Eliot's other poetry, you don't have to be familiar with a particular myth or backstory to access this one. It's interesting to see photographs of East Coker, or to know that Little Gidding was the site of a seventeenth-century religious community, or to realize that some of the references are to wartime bombings in London; but you don't *need* that background to get inside the poem.

It is a BIG poem. It deals with earth, air, fire, and water; grace, faith, hope, and love; beginnings, endings, time, and timelessness. Helen Gardner says that *Four Quartets* is like a piece of music that doesn't represent an object or tell a story; rather it expresses a particular emotion and experience, where the form and the content are in perfect harmony. Near the end of *Four Quartets* is one of my favourite Eliot quotes:

> "We shall not cease from exploration / And the end of all our exploring / Will be to arrive where we started / And know the place for the first time."

Those lines are something like the end of *The Last Battle* (the last book of Narnia), where Jewel the Unicorn says:

> "I have come home at last! This is my real country! I belong here. This is the land I have been looking for all my life, though I never knew it till now…Come further up, come further in!"

At one point in the poem, Eliot talks about saints, people who experience lightning flashes of insight, who have spiritual superpowers. But then he says this:

> For most of us, there is only the unattended
>
> Moment, the moment in and out of time,
>
> The distraction fit, lost in a shaft of sunlight,
>
> The wild thyme unseen, or the winter lightning
>
> Or the waterfall, or music heard so deeply
>
> That it is not heard at all, but you are the music
>
> While the music lasts. These are only hints and guesses,
>
> Hints followed by guesses; and the rest
>
> Is prayer, observance, discipline, thought and action.

I saw an example of this recently on a restaurant television that was showing a hockey game. Someone shot a goal, and everyone was jumping up and down; and then another goal, and everyone was jumping up and down; and another goal, and so on; I thought it must be the most amazing game ever, until I realized they were just showing highlights. We have a tendency in life to focus on the goals and the jumping, and to forget that there's a lot of regular playing going on between them. There's a lot of prayer, observance, discipline, thought, and action that has to happen in our daily lives, in our teaching, in our faith journeys. And for Charlotte Mason educators, there's a lot of habit training, a lot of conscience-educating, a lot of observation and outdoor experience, a lot of learning to read and narrate, lots of things that go on from day to day—and that continue to go on. The upper years of school can be immensely rewarding, but they require even more disciplined work.

Our years of adulthood are also rewarding, but they require daily courage, prayer, thought, and action, if we don't want to end our years like Prufrock. There are amazing moments of grace, but there are also times for just working out our salvation with fear and trembling.

Shall We Follow?

When you're doing school studies of poetry and meter, one of the things not always explained is why a poet *chooses* a particular meter. One of the special things about *Four Quartets*, according to Helen Gardner's book, is that Eliot had moved from using old meters in new ways, as he did in his earlier work, into something quite new that still felt old. Basically, Eliot adopted a four-stress line with a pause in the middle; so, the stresses matter more than the number of syllables. In some places he switches to a three-stress line, sometimes he uses more, but he always comes back to the four-stress pattern. Here's an example from "Burnt Norton," the first of the quartets:

> What might have been and what has been
> Point to one end, which is always present.
> Footfalls echo in the memory
> Down the passage which we did not take
> Towards the door we never opened
> Into the rose-garden. My words echo
> Thus, in your mind.
>   But to what purpose
> Disturbing the dust on a bowl of rose-leaves
> I do not know.
>   Other echoes
> Inhabit the garden. Shall we follow?
> Quick, said the bird, find them, find them,
> Round the corner.

So why does it matter that Eliot, even though he said he was a classicist and a conservative, wanted to move away from a poetic style that seemed trapped in the nineteenth century? According to Russell Kirk, Eliot said that "it was no paradox to be at once an innovator and a reactionary." "Eliot was not breaking tradition but restoring it." He found a new way to talk about "what might have been and what has been," but pointing to "one end, which is always present."

This reminds me, again, of Charlotte Mason. In the Introduction to her *Philosophy of Education*, she singles out a few points that seemed "to differ from general theory and practice": that children should learn by self-effort; that the students would read a large number of set books, literary in style, with studies not chosen on the ground of interest but given consecutively on many subjects; that this would be tested by oral or written narration, so that what the children read they know. She asks there, "has an attempt been made before on a wide scale to secure that scholars should know their books in such a way?" But then, right away, she refers to Francis Bacon and Comenius, who are important names in classical education. You might say that Mason was a classicist who discovered her own meter; that she, like Eliot, was not breaking tradition but restoring it.

You Who Think That You Are Voyaging

At the end of *Four Quartets*, Eliot addresses people on a voyage, and says, *"you are not the same people who left that station,"* and *"You are not those who saw the harbour / Receding, or those who will disembark."*

[As of 2016], I have experienced several endings, beginnings, and other time markers and changes over the last year or two. We ended nineteen years of homeschooling when our youngest daughter entered high school; I published my first book; we changed churches but then went back again; and we're trying to find a new house. We are looking for an ending so that we can have another new beginning.

But I am not the same person I was when I "left the station"; the person who began marriage, who began motherhood, who began homeschooling. I am not even the same person who got on an airplane in Toronto on Wednesday morning. I am not who I will be at the end of my journey...although Eliot cautions us that we may only *think* that we're voyaging, because sometimes we come back around to the place where we began.

Being at a conference can give us a strange sensation of being "other", or out of real time; the routine is different, the beds are different, the food is different, we don't have to do the dishes; many of us are away from our families; we spend these few days like people on a voyage. What we have learned or experienced here may mark the beginning of something new, a new idea or motivation to act. Eliot cautions us not to worry too much about whether our actions will bear fruit, but, as is often said when talking about Charlotte Mason education, we can only sow the seed and trust the process, and know that, as he quotes from Julian of Norwich, that all will be well. Not perfect, not always the way we want things to be, but well.

Here's something to take with you:

> Here between the hither and the farther shore
>
> While time is withdrawn, consider the future
>
> And the past with an equal mind...
>
> (T. S. Eliot, "Little Gidding" in *Four Quartets*)

Breaking Out of Our Raccoons

> A lady at church was asking the kids if they knew how caterpillars turn into butterflies. One little boy called out, "I know! They have to go into raccoons!"
> (Our family blog, 2006)

> ... All my life I've been searching for that crazy missing part
> And with one touch, you just rolled away the stone that held my heart
> And now I see that the answer was as easy, as just asking you in
> And I am so sure I could never doubt your gentle touch again
> It's like the power of the wind...
>
> (Keith Green, "Your Love Broke Through")

Here's a listening assignment for you: check out the February 5, 2025, episode of the PostEverything podcast, titled "Finding Meaning in a Fragmented World." It's an interview between hosts Brad Edwards and John Houmes, and their guest Jake Meador, who is editor-in-chief of *Mere Orthodoxy* (which I misheard as *Neo-Orthodoxy*), and the author of two books on the state of the world and the place of Christians within it.

The short version of the conversation is that people, more than ever, are "desperate to find identity and belonging." They are hungry for something undefined; the "comfortably numb" life is leaving them discombobulated. And what is it that they need? According to the speakers, the answer lies in meaningful connection both with others and with God. Also, in paying attention.

Here's something I transcribed from the podcast:

> When we are constantly pivoting our attention all over the place there's kind of drain you feel by the end of the day. The shut in life becomes easier; you can sit down, turn something on streaming video, make a quick dinner in the kitchen or order something out, and things are not competing for

> your attention. But that is also the time you could meet someone, go for a walk...but you feel mentally tapped out...It's not the same problem that people generations ago faced...but there is something going on here with the capacity of our brain to meaningfully engage with certain things.

Until recently, I might not have understood "make a quick dinner in the kitchen" and "turn something on streaming video" in quite that way. Now that does describe my typical evenings, and, yes, sometimes I do order a container of veggie Lo Mein and then hang out with a Sudoku puzzle. In my own case, the "hard" is the new reality of finding myself alone, which isn't something that everyone experiences; but it does help me to empathize with the more widespread problem. And, if you notice, the first step in the solution to the double-whammy of exhaustion and loneliness—if we had the resources and the energy to access it or create it, which many people don't—would be basic interaction with others, and with the natural world. "Meeting someone" and "going for a walk." But not texting, not social media. What we need here is real fish.

Here's the hard part: even those basic, easy things now need to be created intentionally; but we may be forgetting how to do them, or just not feel up to it. (One of the interviewers said, "Our social muscles are atrophying.") Jake Meador asks, "How do you notice anything outside of yourself when the world is sapping that much of your energy and personal attention?" Well, the truth is mostly that we don't; unless we happen to live in Mitford, where maybe we don't like everybody on our street, but we understand that we're going to interact with them anyway; and our town is our place to belong, whether we would have chosen it or not. Or maybe we live in a town where there's a great homeschooling community, with nature hikes, band classes, and group graduations—but those don't happen automatically, somebody has to start them going.

I grew up in a neighbourhood full of family history, where I could walk or bike to school, church, Brownie meetings, just about everything. We knew not only present-day neighbours, but past ones as well, through our parents' stories, and through the names of streets, parks, even rooms in the church named for members who gave something exceptional of themselves. The church itself was started back when people felt that a neighbourhood without a church was

Breaking Out of Our Raccoons

lacking something vital, so they got busy and built one. We made full use of it: my parents were married there, I was "christened" there, I went to Sunday school and Brownies and youth group there, Bryan and I were married there, my grandparents' funerals were held there. But almost all those people and things are gone now; even the church was sold and the remaining members scattered across other congregations. I have very few places now to go "home." I found it interesting recently to talk to a cousin who grew up somewhere else but who came to visit often enough that she knew many of the things in the neighbourhood, like the corner store across from the church, where we got Popsicles. Sometimes you don't realize how much you've missed those things until you talk to someone else who remembers.

To use a metaphor that just occurred to me (not from the podcast), life for many of us feels—or, rather, un-feels—like a movie scene where someone goes to prison, is stripped of all their personal belongings, and is given very little in return: a blanket, a uniform. In the same way, many of our lives have been stripped of a sense of place, of home, of relationships, and of true purpose. (The podcasters used the word "exile.") Sometimes that's because of actual bad things that have happened, like losing loved ones or having to emigrate. Sometimes it's just the way the world is right now. We work from home or in a place where we don't really talk to co-workers; then we go and work out at a gym; we shop for dinner at a big supermarket, and then, yes, we come home and heat up whatever it is in the microwave. But look, we are living in the world of the golden touchscreen! We have phones, we have games, we have pictures to look at, so we shouldn't be bored and lonely, or wish too much that we had those other things back. So maybe we'll shop—shopping is fun. Maybe we'll scroll. Maybe we'll work, exercise, or self-actualize.

But then what when we can't? (Don't even say if; there's always going to be a when.) What do we do when the money runs out or the people are gone? What are we worth if we can't work...or walk? And who are we, if we don't upload our brunch or vacation or schoolroom photos?

If you think this is a unique situation, you might want to read what Solomon said about "nothing new under the sun." But it seems worse today. Harder. We've spent most of our knowing-ourselves-and-what-makes-life-worth-living capital, and those coming after us are starting out with less than nothing. No neighbourhood with grandparents around the corner; no church where your parents were married; maybe even no Popsicles. It may not seem to matter that much, until it isn't there; and a whole society missing out on "there" equals a lot of unhappy people.

"How Dare You Open a Spaceman's Helmet on an Uncharted Planet?"

The podcast conversation then turns to what we experience in our attempts to connect with the Christian church, which can vary widely (or should it be wildly?) depending on both what a particular church offers, and the expectations we bring ourselves. Are we really connecting with God, or just with other human beings—and is that necessarily a bad thing, if we're disconnected from both God and people? Is the emphasis on doctrines to believe, or on "nourishing your spiritual potential?" How does the church affirm or question who we believe we are? If someone yanks off our space helmet, will we be able to breathe on this planet? What if we have to admit that we're just a toy? Worse...what if we're a broken toy?

Jake Meador surprised me at this point by casually referring to Charlotte Mason's use of the word "atmosphere," and things that are "caught rather than taught." So, let's talk about atmosphere. Can the concept of atmosphere itself be caught rather than taught, if it's even something that *can* be taught? This is what I mean: consider that you have a six-volume set of Mason's writings, and you want to know what she said about atmosphere. You would probably start by using the index, or the table of contents. You could, of course, just do an online search, and you should be able to come up with a decent working definition of "atmosphere" (vs. "environment"), without even taking your helmet off. Here's something to get you started:

> The bracing atmosphere of truth and sincerity
> should be perceived in every school; and here again
> the common pursuit of knowledge by teacher and
> class comes to our aid and creates a current of fresh
> air perceptible even to the chance visitor...We
> foresee happy days for children when all teachers
> know that no other exciting motive whatever is
> necessary to produce good work in each individual

Breaking Out of Our Raccoons

of however big a class than that love of knowledge which is natural to every child. (*Philosophy of Education*, pp. 97–98)

So, we're looking for something simple and natural, like a breath of fresh air. But how do we get it? Are there specific how-to's and instructions? Is there a checklist or cheat sheet of C. M. atmosphere protocols somewhere out there? A rubric to evaluate how well your atmosphere lines up with the average C. M. household? An alarm system to say that you're overbalanced and have too much atmosphere and not enough discipline or life? These days, I wouldn't be too sure that even such a silly thing doesn't exist, if someone could make it and market it. But no, don't go looking for one.

Here's a better way, once you've got the basic definition down. Like Arnold Bennett recommending Hazlitt and Browning, I will offer a double prescription. First, read some part of Mason's books that isn't specifically about atmosphere—but look for atmosphere in it. I recommend the five chapters grouped as "Parents in Council" in *Formation of Character*, especially the dinner-party conversations. Of course, you can kill all the C. M. birds with one stone and look for examples of "discipline" and "life" as well, but that's optional.

Second, do what Mason herself liked to do, and read a biography or novel that follows a character from childhood through adulthood, noting down instances of positive or negative atmosphere, especially in the person's young years. Was the family (or school) atmosphere-thermostat set too high or too low, so that they were raised in either a stifling "hothouse" atmosphere, or one with too little guidance and protection? Did someone try to change the atmosphere, for better or worse? How did that work out? You may start noticing how the atmosphere in your own home seems a little too weighed down (do you need to declutter some of the toys?). Or you realize that you haven't been making time to pray and read Scripture together, but soon it's going to be Advent, and there's your perfect time to get a nightly gathering back on track. Or you see that everybody's stressed at the dinner table, for whatever reason, and that you need to work at putting more enjoyment back into that time. (Simpler foods? No-spill cups? No devices at the table?) Small changes, right? And that's how to let the idea of atmosphere itself be "caught" rather than "taught."

So, what does what we know about atmosphere have to do with the ideas in the podcast? I think the connection is finding that "breath of fresh air" in a church, something almost unintentional that draws people in and makes them want to stay—or run for the hills. We don't want a cold atmosphere, of course; but a too-smothering welcome can be scary. Too bright and loud, or too quiet and dull? Annoyed faces in the pews when your children make a little noise, or helpful offers of sermon colouring pages? (Maybe colouring pages aren't your thing, but it's the thought.)

Don't mistake style for atmosphere. Remember how the podcast started? People are disenchanted, missing out, hungry for something more; and if it's there, they'll hear it, even if you're meeting in a school gymnasium with a struggling music team and an improvised Sunday school space. Maybe your church uses the King James Bible, or you pray with thees and thous; maybe some of your songs are in another language; don't try to change just for the sake of change. "Contemporary" is not always necessary; "listening" and "caring" and "presenting the Gospel" *are*, no matter what the denomination. Meador contrasts churches that emphasize a "cool show for irreligious people" with those that use traditional liturgy and expect new people to catch on as they stick around, perhaps offering a gentle introduction to what is unfamiliar.

> "This is sure a different kind of church for us...I don't know if we can keep up with th' way y'all do things."
>
> Wayne nodded, clearly in agreement.
>
> "We need to have some lessons on the prayer book," said the vicar. "Would be good for everybody. What about a covered dish next Sunday? Followed by a discussion on how we do things?" In his new parish, there would be no slacking; it was fish or cut bait.
> (Jan Karon, *Light from Heaven*)

It seems then that this thing we call atmosphere in the church needs...more welcoming. More explaining, when it's time for explaining. And more potlucks. But, the interviewers ask Meador: who does the welcoming, who creates this "rarefied" atmosphere, when so many Christians find it a bit scarce in our own lives? And what makes the experience of church any different from other places where we might look for social, moral, or emotional support? The rest of the podcast attempts to answer that question, and I won't try to cover it all here, except to say that the church should help us find our place in God's story (instead of trying to shoehorn Him into ours). Here's one way to think about that:

> At least once every day I shall look steadily up at the sky and remember that I, a consciousness with a conscience, am on a planet traveling in space with wonderfully mysterious things above and about me...Even if I turn out to be wrong, I shall bet my life on the assumption that this world is not idiotic, neither run by an absentee landlord, but that today, this very day, some stroke is being added to the cosmic canvas that in due course I shall understand with joy as a stroke made by the architect who calls himself Alpha and Omega. (Clyde Kilby)

The conclusion is that our minds, bodies, and spirits need to meaningfully engage with our planet and the other beings on it, not to mention the "wonderfully mysterious things above and about [us]." That, as Keith Green said, is the answer to the "crazy missing part."

Fish Or Cut Bait

I mentioned earlier that I now live in an apartment. The main reason for this location, besides being handy for shopping and such, was that it is very close to the church where we started making ourselves at home a few years ago. If I tell you some of the things I've signed up for this fall, will you understand that I'm not at all listing them to make myself sound good? They're just examples of things that maybe people can do who have been blessed with the time to do them.

> Helping with English as a Second Language classes
>
> Handing out canned food in the church parking lot (the local food bank sends a mobile truck and church members help out)
>
> Taking a six-week class about faith and the arts
>
> Making cookies and helping set up for a holiday event, although I probably won't be attending it. (Seasonal frolics are not my best thing right now.)
>
> Getting involved with a new Bible study group when

Borrowed Riches

the other class is over.

But the apartment itself is also a place for encounters, even brief ones, and in that I am often reminded of Bryan's stories of the dog-walkers. This morning I took the elevator down to the laundry room, put in two loads, and when I came back to check, one of them was still dry—the phone app said the cycle was done, but no. When I pushed the start button again, off it went. A lady folding her laundry commiserated, "Well, that puts your laundry behind another half hour." I said I didn't really mind, it wasn't a day to be in a hurry. When I was heading back down to check on that, half an hour later, an elderly lady got on, and I said hello. She told me about her back pain, saying, "Sometimes I cry." But there was the ground floor, and she was getting out: "I'm sorry," was all I could offer, but I meant it.

I returned to the basement in a little while, moved the wet laundry to a dryer, and headed back upstairs. Another woman got on, holding a couple of potatoes in her hand. "Just don't ask about the potatoes," she said as she got off.

Well, that made three people to talk to in under an hour, all because a washing machine didn't function right. I will pray for the lady with the sore back. But I guess I may never know about the potatoes.

There are also some things I want to do more of, that I need to remind myself are better options for connecting with the world than leftover Lo Mein and Sudoku. Here's a list:

> Get outside more, preferably with movement attached, even when the season gets cold and dark. Sitting on the balcony gets only half credit.
>
> Learn more about a few life skills that don't make my heart spin, but that I need to know anyway. Share what I'm learning with anyone else who could use that information.
>
> Read some of the poetry books I've been collecting, with a glance every so often at William Hazlitt.
>
> Take more photographs of clouds, but also of the things on the ground.
>
> Pray more for people around me. People on the elevator. People in the laundry room. People sitting by themselves at church. People lined up for canned

beans. Artsy people, baking people, beginning-English people, Bible-study people, tree-decorating people.

One Potato, Two Potato

What's in your fridge? was a conversation question in one of the ESL lessons. We went around the circle and people answered, "Chinese cabbage." "Rice." "Eggs and vegetables." I said, "Leftovers," which was pretty much true, although that didn't include the bag of red potatoes that had been hanging out in the crisper for a few days, alongside two sweet potatoes. It didn't include the jars of apple butter and salsa, the two eggs and the half liter of milk, or the half-container of cream cheese. It would have included two Gala apples, but I had just baked those into a cake (along with some of the apple butter) because a friend was coming to visit.

Until last summer, our refrigerator typically had a large container of milk, a bag of beef thawing for goulash, and multiple bottles of barbecue sauce, sauerkraut, and jam, along with orange juice and Diet Pepsi. It always held baskets of cold cuts and cheese for sandwiches, because Bryan loved them. But I don't eat a lot of sandwiches. Sometimes I don't even buy bread. Shocking.

My apartment fridge is pretty bare right now, not because I don't have money for food, but because I'm not always sure how to keep the right amount of everything in there for one person. Also, I have to remember to go buy the food, which sounds obvious, but, because I was married to someone who liked making random grocery stops, often things would magically appear in our fridge. A box of apples from the farm stand; a bag of salad to eat with the goulash; cheese danishes for weekend breakfast. Now it's on me to make the magic, and sometimes I just don't feel like bothering.

But as our friend Wendi used to say, what's in your hand? After that ESL class, I looked in the almost-empty fridge again and thought, "Potato soup in the slow cooker, with the red potatoes and sweet potatoes cut up together, and a bit of frozen onion and peppers. I could stir in the bit of squash soup from yesterday's lunch, and that last bit of cream cheese. And eat it with one of the lentil burritos I made and froze last weekend." Suddenly that sounded like a good autumn meal instead of just a random bag of potatoes. (And it was.)

So, what does all that have to do with anything? I think it's this: that maybe you are teaching your children at home, and you're new at this. Or you're moving to Charlotte Mason from some other teaching method. Maybe you've decided to trim things down; or circumstances are dictating a simpler season whether you want it or not.

In any case, what you have in the curriculum fridge is what you have. It may not look like what you're used to. It might seem like too much, or not enough. You might wish that a magic homeschooling fairy would supply every link and picture and explanation you need, plus cheese danishes; but you might also realize that—strangely enough—your kids are doing fine, and you're learning more yourself.

Over a decade ago, I wrote a blog post about making the most of limited homeschooling resources, and these were my rules:

> 1. Use what you have.
> 2. Use what you have creatively.
> 3. Stay aware of your "big picture." Unless you're naturally serene about letting the unschooling chips fall where they may, you need to keep evaluating, planning, trying to keep in mind whatever educational goals or philosophy you steer by. Plus whatever family circumstances, special needs, etc. you have to deal with.
> 4. In other words, you can use what you have, or what comes your way, as long as it fits into your overall education plan.

I suggested a "what's in your hand" exercise of pretending (or maybe it's not pretending at all) that you are limited to just a few books and resources.

> From very loose planning ("read the book"), to more structured copywork and dictation, notebooking, dramatizations, or complete unit studies, how many ways can you think of to get the most out of this resource? If it's a map, are there ways you could add tags or markings to illustrate something you're studying? If it's a math activity book, which activities can you honestly imagine doing, and (just as important), which ones will provide the strongest learning experiences for your children? You can take any worthwhile book as far as you like, use it as far as you can, and it won't cost you any extra.

I asked—fortuitously, since we've been talking about poetry here already—how you could similarly approach a book of poems.

> Can you use it for reading? Writing? Creative narration? Nature notebooking? Music, if the poems have been set to music (or you're very talented yourself, or your children are)?

> Can your students plan a "poetry concert," just for your family or for others as well? Or you can read a poem slowly and carefully, maybe taking turns on stanzas, copying or memorizing favourite lines.

What are you going to eat today? Go to your fridge, see what's there, and put it in the blender or the pan. Maybe you'll make a mediocre kale smoothie. But maybe you'll invent a great two-potato soup. Some days are just like that.

Believe It or Not, It's Just Me

I am a Canadian, so the word "liberty" doesn't resonate as patriotically for me as it does for my American friends; but most of us, no matter where we're from, think that "liberty" is a good thing. Constitutions and charters can explain liberty, but they can't create it or give it—we already have it. As St. Paul wrote, liberty means "plant[ing] your feet therefore within the freedom that Christ has won for us." (Galatians 5:1, Phillips translation). It means living as if you've been given the red superhero suit, with or without the flying manual. As if you're allowed to—in fact, required to—make choices, no matter what the circumstances. To choose courage, calm, and creativity over a dull, scared-to-eat-a-peach life.

Charlotte Mason called that the way of the will.

A friend told me recently that when stressful situations come up at work, she has decided to act rather than react. She said she was inspired by a sermon about the prophet Elijah who was cared for by God in a drought-ridden land. One might say that he was living in an oasis; but also that his life was a kind of oasis to those around him. I also read somewhere that faith is not about filling your own cup (so that you can, theoretically, pour out generously to others), but about living obediently, and letting God worry about how full the cup gets. And if that's His concern, not ours, then, yes, we are free to make choices.

Borrowed Riches

Which brings us to some helpful books about living with liberty and will, in our families, in our churches, in our own lives. This short list doesn't exclude others, I'm just pulling up a few that I'm most familiar with: Charlotte Mason's *Ourselves*, Kendra Adachi's *Lazy Genius Way*; Cindy Rollins's *Mere Motherhood* and *Beyond Mere Motherhood*; Edith Schaeffer's *What is a Family* and *Hidden Art of Homemaking*; Susan Schaeffer Macaulay's *For the Family's Sake*. (Yes, I said *Family's*, not *Children's*. Not everybody knows there's a sequel, and if you haven't read it, you should.)

A book that is new to me is Emily Freeman's *The Next Right Thing*. In one of the chapters, the author feels overwhelmed while shopping at a garden center, because she knows little about choosing plants. She describes the anxious thoughts running through her mind: how does she even have the right to be there, acting like she has a clue how to choose between one succulent and another? Is somebody going to ask for her plant-raising credentials? What if she makes a terrible choice? But then she reminds herself (and us):

> Having pretty flowers, painting a room a bold color, or trying out a new recipe is not reserved for people who know more, who have more, or who seem to be more than you. This is for you too. You don't have to be fancy, rich, chosen, or special. You just get to be you. You are allowed to take up space in the room. You are allowed to choose something and you are allowed to change your mind. While I am standing here looking at plants, a phrase arrives in my mind complete, like a green leaf falling onto the grass in summer. Pick what you like, then see how it grows.

Which brings us back to liberty. Charlotte Mason would add something else: principles. Also, if there's an ethical aspect involved, an educated conscience. That's it; that's all you need. Go to the garden center, choose your succulents, be polite to the cashier, and have a nice day.

But did you notice Freeman's phrase "you are allowed to change your mind?" That one can be a bit mind-blowing for some of us, especially if we think we've packed all those principles in our handbag and so we are now magically equipped to make the right choices, and even that we had *better* make those perfect choices, because we know the perfect things are out there, and if we don't find them the first time, we've failed. Or we blame the choices themselves.

We decide that Mason must have been wrong about the ways she taught spelling, because our kids are pushing back about copywork and dictation; and we think that homeschooling itself is something we'll never be much good at.

We're sure we'll never grow a successful garden, because we don't have fancy tools and we're not sure how deep to plant the different kinds of seeds, or what all those kinds of tomatoes are.

We think we should buy one of those style apps that tells us our best colours, because we never took art and don't know our hue from our chroma, so how are we supposed to know what shade of blue sweater suits us best? There's a Youtuber who posts about dressing like a chic French lady, and she has a simple solution for that last one: go to the mirror, hold it up. Do you like it? There you go.

Sometimes we haven't made a wrong choice; we just need to get to know the terrain a little better. As Freeman says further on, there are always things in life that we think everybody else knows and that we're embarrassed to admit don't come naturally to us. Some things are going to take us longer, and we are going to make mistakes, sometimes truly dumb mistakes. Louisa May Alcott's novel *Jack and Jill* is about a group of young friends who, like the sisters in *Little Women*, make resolutions to be more cheerful and patient, or more helpful at home. A lot of their early efforts backfire. One girl gives her little brother a cold bath which causes him to catch croup; another tries to redecorate and sets the curtains on fire. We may feel like beginners in whatever we're doing for a very long season; but when we look back, like these same girls later in the novel, we may realize how far we've come.

Even then, we can choose wrong, and we probably will. Just because we have principles and the Holy Spirit doesn't mean we're going to do everything right the first time. What we don't want is to be tied up in knots, unable to make any choice at all because we're afraid of failing, of displeasing people, or of disappointing the selves we wish we were.

Freeman also makes a final point that hits close to home for me:

> I know this little story is only a small example of all the ways you may be starting over, starting again, or starting out for the first time. No matter the size or scope, new beginnings always come with a mix of all kinds of emotions.

Borrowed Riches

Her prayer at the end of the chapter is about finding courage and patience, pace and grace to make choices: important ones, and seemingly unimportant ones. Sometimes small decisions can cause as much emotional struggle as big ones. In the past few weeks, I've bought a lipliner, a dustmop, a copy of Richard Wilbur's poems, a navy winter coat, and a computer printer (not to mention a grave marker).

The poetry book was an easy choice.

The lipliner was a bit of a wild card, because I couldn't try it on first. I just had to "pick one and see how it grows." And it was fine.

I found two navy coats at the first store I went to, and the only real decision was the shorter or the longer version.

The dustmop, however, caused some decision fatigue, which I put down to the fact that Bryan usually picked out our household cleaning equipment. How was I supposed to know what the apartment floors were made of? Did I want a spinning mop, or a taco-shaped one? A wet one or a dry one? In the end, I walked over to Walmart and picked a basic do-it-all mop from the aisle with the back-to-college supplies.

And if you think I now have any expertise in ordering grave markers, I don't, because it's not information I'm hoping to have to use again anytime soon. The emotions around that are not about the specific decisions, but rather the hard privilege, though also the responsibility, of making such a decision at all. Here's an example that more of us can relate to: how are you going to teach your children? It's just as awesome a responsibility. If God has called you to do this, then you do "belong in the room." But don't wait for a homeschooling fairy to show up and hand you everything. Choose your plan. Put it into action. Trust Him to give the increase.

And cherish your liberty.

The Will and the Wisdom

In a recent blog post called "The Truth in View," Alan Jacobs adroitly combines discussion of two poems by Richard Wilbur, the book of Job, a Shakespearean proverb, Dorothy Sayers' translation of *The Song of Roland*, and something about looking at an onion. That is not pretentious; it's simply plundering the storehouse, and it's one of the reasons I enjoy Jacobs' writing.

"Eyes and No-Eyes"

One of the Wilbur poems discussed is called "Lying." (Jacobs includes only part of it in his post, so you may want to look for the full text elsewhere.) One part of it says:

> All these things
> Are there before us; there before we look
> Or fail to look; there to be seen or not
> By us, as by the bee's twelve thousand eyes,
> According to our means and purposes.

Jacobs picks up on this thought and says, "The key phrase is 'All these things / Are there before us.' We must simply discover the will and the wisdom to recognize what is already present to us." Do you hear some of Eliot's *Four Quartets* in that? Or Charles Kingsley's wresting of natural history from random scratches in rocks, in *Madam How and Lady Why*? Or maybe something by one of the AO Advisory?

> Knowledge predates us. In the sense that it all comes from God, it was here from the beginning. I note that Wordsworth took care to qualify that our existence is new, and that our affinities fit us, in our newness, to existing things. We are materialistic by nature: we want to own things. Regardless, I begin to suspect that the relationships we form to knowledge do not make it belong to us, **but rather bring us to belong to what was here all along**. (Lynn Bruce, in an article on the AO website; bolds mine)

As we learn to care about various things—things of the natural world or personal virtues such as

> honesty—our feelings will motivate us to act
> because of what we know. In this way, knowledge
> becomes virtue in a person's life. (Karen Glass, *In
> Vital Harmony*)

We have been given what we need. Even in less-than-ideal circumstances, we always have more around us, to notice, to wonder at, and to be thankful for, than we first thought.

But without "will and wisdom," we get "Lying." Words that lie do not always begin with vicious intent. Sometimes they come from just speaking or writing down the easy thing, the cliché, the quick conclusion, the clever but meaningless phrase. And what is often the cause of that? "[We] fail to look," as Wilbur says; we don't pay close enough attention. When I was homeschooling, I often heard about Kerry Ruef's *The Private Eye*, a curriculum where children are given a jeweler's loupe which magnifies everything five times larger than normal. The students look at an object through the magic "eye," and draw whatever it is just as they see it, which is science (and maybe art); but they also say, "this is like…" and "that reminds me of…" which is a foundation for poetry. It seems to me, however, that the most important thing taught, or caught, by this process would be truth. Or Truth. And when we recognize Truth, we can also understand and practice generosity. I will talk about that in the Epilogue, but here's a quote that shows what I mean:

> On a recent camping trip a local pastor noticed
> a Clapham Upper School student
> reading Boethius. Though he commented on the
> difficulty of the text, he was more surprised that this
> student not only understood the thesis, but
> delighted in sharing it. (Clapham School website)

Lost Keys

In "Lying," Wilbur calls the human desire to create truth with simile and metaphor "something [that is] in us." He also says that, ever since the Fall, our "simplicity of wish and will" have been "mislaid." Consider that last word. What happens when something important is mislaid? We set everything else aside to look for it. In this case, however, it may not be a matter of just retracing steps through the house and trying to remember where we put our keys. (I found mine yesterday still hanging from the apartment door keyhole, because I had come inside with too many things in my hands and never pulled them out. Very silly of me.)

In this life, we may find only fragments of what we're looking for; but recognizing the urge to search is the first step. Theologically, it may be like that amazing story Lucy reads in *The Voyage of the Dawn-Treader*, that she can never remember afterwards. It's something like Eliot's lines: "Quick, said the bird, find them, find them, / Round the corner." C. S. Lewis also refers to this thing we hear bits of or feel snatches of as "Joy," something he first recognized while reading a poem about the death of the Norse god Baldur.

Wilbur happens to agree with that literary direction:

> It is a chant
>
> Of the first springs, and it is tributary
>
> To the great lies told with the eyes half-shut
>
> That have the truth in view: the tale of Chiron
>
> Who, with sage head, wild heart, and planted hoof
>
> Instructed brute Achilles in the lyre,
>
> Or of the garden where we first mislaid
>
> Simplicity of wish and will, forgetting
>
> Out of what cognate splendor all things came
>
> To take their scattering names...

To apply Wilbur's phrasing to our earlier discussion of mythology, we might say that myths are "great lies told with the eyes half-shut / That have the truth in view." And when we observe things closely, as we might through the jeweler's loupe, when we describe them accurately and unscatter their names, we are not playing the role of "Giant Analysis," but that of his brother "Synthesis" (in *Madam How and Lady Why*). When we create poetic imagery, we are not misleading or mislaying, we are bringing things back together; we are finding. We are not "lying," we are truth-telling with eyes half-shut (partly, as Jacobs says, so that we can more carefully consider our response); and we are participating in all that has come before. Age, social standing, and century of birth are unimportant; what matters is our born-personhood. This is why children's art and music, if created with "the truth in view", matter immensely; and why even a tentative line of poetry feeds back into the whole river (to use Wilbur's image).

And we do it with what Edna St. Vincent Millay calls a "passion that stretches us apart."

> Long have I known a glory in it all,
>
>> But never knew I this;
>
>> Here such a passion is
>
> As stretcheth me apart...
>
> (from "God's World")

Look What the Universe Gave Us

There's a video clip of Paul Williams recalling his writing of the song "Rainbow Connection" for The Muppet Movie. Williams says that he thought he had written himself into a corner by declaring, in the first lines, that rainbows are just rainbows and that's all. He then says, "But look what the universe gave us," and tells how he was able to shift perspective onto a banjo-playing frog who saw greater meaning in rainbows.

Like the insights made (or given) while songwriting.
Like mythology, heroes, poetry, metaphor.

> ...literature is still doing the same job that
> mythology did earlier, but filling in its huge cloudy
> shapes with sharper lights and deeper shadows.
> (Northrop Frye, *The Educated Imagination*)

I want to go back to Richard Wilbur's two phrases: the "something in us" desire to create metaphor and simile, which he says we do have; and the "simplicity of wish and will," which we don't. I think the way they fit together is that our desire to seek out and create beauty comes from our sense of that missing piece. But what does he mean by "simplicity of wish and will?" It is obviously something that our first parents had in Eden, during the days of first relationships with everything around them, when there was no temptation, no complication, no distraction. The word "cognate" that Wilbur uses means connection, commonality, cousin-ship; and "cognate splendor" suggests even more life and brilliance; not just everyday glory (if there is such a thing), but the "This" of Millay, or the "Joy" of Lewis.

In an earlier book, *Offering Ourselves*, I included Elizabeth Goudge's words about the rue plant:

> ...Astringent—that means contraction. Bitter to the taste. Repentant. Compassionate... Single-mindedness... Contraction. Everything gathered in for the giving of yourself. The whole of you. Nothing kept back. (*Pilgrim's Inn*)

I also wrote this about it:

> Mason's [philosophy] is all about what some people call mindfulness: *being* whenever and wherever you are, doing what you are supposed to be doing. Reading, practicing, chopping firewood, listening to a customer's complaint, playing with your children, sailing a boat, balancing an account, watching ants, planning a battle, praying. And resting fully in between.

That echoes a passage from C. S. Lewis which I had planned to use as an opening quote for this book, except that I wasn't sure how the bomb imagery would come across. Please read it here in the spirit that Lewis intended:

> If we are all going to be destroyed by an atomic bomb, let that bomb when it comes find us doing sensible and human things: praying, working, teaching, reading, listening to music, bathing the children, playing tennis, chatting to our friends over a pint and a game of darts—not huddled together like frightened sheep and thinking about bombs. They may break our bodies (a microbe can do that) but they need not dominate our minds. ("On Living in an Atomic Age," 1948)

This speaks not only to our lost "simplicity of wish and will," but to Will itself, capital W. Will is what allows humans to work, pray, declutter, and even drink and play games in the shadow of wars, or through an autumn season of personal grief. Like the furry Hrossa of Malacandra (Lewis, *Out of the Silent Planet*), our lives should be concerned with fishing, or whatever makes up our working days, but also with more than fishing. Like the Hrossa, we are also sustained by song, story, poetry, lament, celebration, worship; and these things always work best in family, in community.

The astringent, "lost simplicity" part—stay with me here—means that we, in every sense, declutter. We pull back from the just-okay, the dollar-store cupboard-fillers, the bargain ideas we grab as they flutter by—including enslaving emotions and taunting voices from inside our heads—to allow vocational and relational things their full time and meaning. Turning our eyes from the gate crashers and towards the important thing that got mislaid, but that we know is still there if we look for it—that is how we can connect the scattered pieces of creation and become less scattered ourselves. (Because education is a science of relations.)

Lest you think that I am overstretching what Richard Wilbur meant in "Lying"—it's just a poem, after all—you might be interested in what he himself said about it, some years ago, in an interview with Arlo Haskell:

> **Haskell**: At our 2003 Seminar, you read "Lying" and called it both one of your best and one of your most difficult-to-understand poems. Would you agree with [Wallace] Stevens that poetry should "make the visible a little hard to see"?
>
> **Wilbur**: The main thing that "Lying" has to say is that we can't create another reality, because all things are inevitably part of the "cognate splendor" of the original creation and its development...I don't think that, in Stevens's phrase, my poem "makes the visible a little hard to see": the likening of onion skin to sail, for instance, is meant to be vivid. If my wife's first reaction to "Lying" was "at last you've written a poem that's unintelligible from beginning to end," she soon came to see that the poem is a bombardment of proofs that the world is one.
>
> **Haskell**: Your poems maintain such good will. Are you an optimist by nature?
>
> **Wilbur**: If an optimist is somebody who thinks everything will come out all right, I'm not. But, if it's optimistic to think that the world is fundamentally a great wonder and a great order, yes, I subscribe to those things.

"The likening of onion skin to sail, for instance, is meant to be vivid." Maybe we do create with our eyes half shut; but we want those who will listen or look to open their own eyes wide. Not concealing but making things plain. Offering order. Good will. Proof "that the world is one." And wonder.

This is what we need to search for, even if we pull the apartment apart looking for it, even if it takes a lifetime. But maybe we'll find it, in the end, hanging from the doorknob where it's been all along.

A Postscript

In the blog post, Alan Jacobs says:

> Wilbur is talking about *The Song of Roland* of course, and these words, coming at the end of the poem, tell us of two ways of shaming the devil: to be "faithful unto death" in one's *deeds* and in one's *words*.

And that may be a perfect way to state the goal of Charlotte Mason's vision of a lifelong education. We want to live, as long as we live, in such a way that our actions and our words demonstrate faithfulness to our Creator, the one whose name is written on our hearts, as well as the bottoms of our feet.

Epilogue: "What Autumn Leaves Disclose"

I have another media assignment for you: to find and watch Malcolm Guite's YouTube video titled "'And Is It Not Enough?' My own Autumn poem." In it, Guite refers to two famous autumn poems by Keats and Shelley, and points out how the best poetry is not, so to speak, an armchair activity. He says:

> Autumn is richer for me because of those two poems. Keats alerts me to the mists, to the mellow fruitfulness, to the plumping of the kernels, to the moss, cottage, trees. My eyes are opened...This is what Coleridge says poetry does. It removes the film of familiarity. It awakens us to wonder.

Guite goes on to say that he had hesitated to write an autumn poem himself, because Keats and Shelley said so much already about autumn's beautiful colours and its wild winds; its joyful time of harvest but also its darker grieving as the leaves drop and the nights lengthen. Then he saw that his admiration of those poems, and his hesitancy to write his own, raised a question that could be answered poetically. He asks in the video,

> Why do I read [their poems]? And why do I hope that somebody might get something from reading what I've written?...[because there is an] extraordinary thing that a poem does...it is [as Cardinal] Newman used to say, "Cor ad cor loquitur": it's heart speaking unto heart. The poem makes this extraordinary and miraculous bridge between the inside islanded consciousness of one person, the inner view of that person, and gives it as a gift to the inside consciousness of another person. And to do that is miraculous.

"Cor ad cor loquitur." "The poem makes this extraordinary and miraculous bridge between the inside islanded consciousness of one person...and another person." Where have we heard something like that before?

> Our children...live, that is, the common life, and are

Epilogue: "What Autumn Leaves Disclose"

not stranded in an inlet of individual culture.
(*Formation of Character*, p. 302)

We have explored our own Mansouls; but we are also challenged to build bridges to others. The bridge-building does not exclude those who don't paint or write poetry or compose music, or even those who don't feel they could explain or teach it as well as people who do literature podcasts. Yes, being a poet, Malcolm Guite did take that step of writing his own response in verse; but that is not the only way, or even the best way to share the common life, for most of us. Just walking and reading and talking and looking and listening together is also enough.

> And thou shalt teach them diligently unto thy children, and shalt talk of them when thou sittest in thine house, and when thou walkest by the way, and when thou liest down, and when thou risest up.
> (Deuteronomy 6:7)

Over-Plus-Ness

Just before reading his own poem "And Is It Not Enough?", Guite plays with language a bit:

> ... it's about the over-plus-ness, the over-brim that both autumn and poetry offer us, and about celebrating that, and saying there's always more.

This jogged my memory because I had just read something on a similar theme by Brandy Vencel:

> I once heard a complaint about Charlotte Mason education. The person liked the idea of it but didn't like that there was so much study that seemed to be required. Can't we just buy some books and read them? What's the big deal? Well, in a sense, yes, we can just buy some books and read them with our students, but one of the things that sets Mason apart is that she seemed to think that the best teachers, her teachers, teach from overflow.
> (*Aftercast*, Episode 23)

So, let's break this down a bit.
Malcolm Guite wrote his autumn poem from overflow; there was

so much happening in his mind that it had to come out. Autumn, in all its wild winds and blue skies and corn and dying leaves, is a season of "the over-plus-ness, the over-brim." I think that means, to use a biblical image, something pressed down and running over, too much to be contained in an ordinary jar. Perhaps a good autumn image for it is the cornucopia, the horn of plenty. In our family, it was lots of whipped cream squirted on the Thanksgiving pumpkin pie. These are things that celebrate always-more-ness.

Poetry itself, the best poetry, is also a thing of "over-plus-ness." It is too real to be experienced only while sitting at a classroom desk or in a comfortable chair, and too big to be kept to oneself. To return to mythology, think of Baucis and Philemon, who are known for their wish to be together in death as well as in life. But there was a second gift from the gods with whom they had shared their supper: their small hut was turned into a temple, and, in Hawthorne's words, they were told to "Exercise your hospitality in yonder palace as freely as in the poor hovel to which you welcomed us last evening."

Of course, generous hospitality sounds easy if you have a beautiful temple and a magic self-filling pitcher; but that is exactly what we do have. We have the world and all that's in it, the summer and autumn, the clouds and oceans and snow and trees, with the Creator's name Sharpied all over them and written on our hearts as well. We have writers and artists who have tried to describe it in words, paint, music, sculpture, dance, many of them most admirably. But "is it not enough?" asks Malcolm Guite. No, not quite…because we each have a part to play as well.

"So I must try," he says in his poem, "In my poor turn, to help you see it too… / That autumn might unfold again in you, / Feeling with me what falling leaves disclose."

This and More

Many years ago, I read Susan Cooper's fantasy novel *The Grey King*. In a key scene, young Will Stanton is commanded to answer a riddle: "Who were the three generous men of the Island of Britain?" Will, having been granted an exceptional knowledge of such things, digs through his memory, and then says boldly, "The three generous men of the Island of Britain. Nudd the Generous, son

Epilogue: "What Autumn Leaves Disclose"

of Senllyt. Mordaf the Generous, son of Serwan. Rhydderch the Generous, son of Tydwal Tudglyd. *And Arthur himself was more generous than the three."*

Now, first, I didn't know that Cooper did not make up that triad of names—they're part of a very old British tradition. Second, that didn't sound like any kind of riddle I had ever heard; I thought riddles were meant to be funny, and it wasn't especially funny. And third, I wondered about that word "generous." "Generous" as in "they gave great birthday presents" didn't seem meaningful enough for this scene.

It turns out that I was right. Yes, "generosity" means a willingness to give of oneself and one's possessions; and it means an ability to go beyond one's own desires, for instance "generously" forgiving someone for a wrong. But its early meaning is closer to other words that English also borrowed from Latin and Old French, such as "gentility" and "gentlemen." The word has its roots in the Latin *genus*, referring to one's stock or race—so, well-born, noble, and possessing the characteristics that were believed to belong to a person of such birth, such as courage, honour, kindness, gentleness. In short, magnanimity (with one distinction which we'll get to in a minute).

So, when Mason states, not just once but twice in her principles of education, that children should have a generous curriculum, is she perhaps saying not just that they should have teetering stacks of schoolbooks, and freedom to roam through the storehouse, but that they need a *curriculum based on generosity*?

> All roads lead to Rome, and all I have said is meant to enforce the fact that much and varied humane reading, as well as human thought expressed in the forms of art, is, not a luxury, a tit-bit, to be given to children now and then, but their very bread of life, which they must have in abundant portions and at regular periods. This and more is implied in the phrase, "The mind feeds on ideas and therefore children should have a generous curriculum."
> (*Philosophy of Education*, p. 111)

"This and more." Yes, we want to keep these children well fed, we want to be as generous to them as we can; but we also want them to have minds and hearts that give to others out of that abundance. And why? Later in that book she refers to John Milton, who said that "a complete and generous education" is "that which fits a man to perform justly, skilfully and magnanimously all the offices both private and public of peace and war." (p. 249)

To go even further, Mason wrote a whole chapter on "Generosity" in *Ourselves*, in which she acknowledges the noble roots of the word, but makes it clear that it is essential for everyone.

> At first sight it seems as if Generosity were not a Lord in every bosom, but ruled only the noblest hearts; but this is not the fact...The nature of Generosity is to bring forth, to give, always at the cost of personal suffering or deprivation, little or great. (p. 103)

She not only notes the connection to Magnanimity, but adds a distinction:

> ...what Magnanimity is to the things of the mind, Generosity is to the things of the heart...It is a certain large trustfulness in his dealings, rather than the largeness of his gifts, or the freedom of his outlay, that marks the generous man... There are so many great things to care about that [the generous person] has no mind and no time for the small frettings of life; his concerns are indeed great, for what concerns man concerns him. (pp. 104-105)

We do often use the word "magnanimous" to describe generous acts, so perhaps the lines between them don't have to be strictly defined. However, what is more important here is something that brings us back to the Three Generous Men. Generosity is not "the largeness of [a person's] gifts, or the freedom of his outlay," Mason says; it is instead "a certain large trustfulness in his dealings."

As magnanimity keeps our minds gainfully occupied, generosity keeps our hearts so busy that we don't have time to feel offended, resentful, or, just possibly, anxious. Generosity gives at a personal cost, but out of a firm belief that God will make up the difference one way or another.

Gathered In

In *The Magician's Nephew*, Digory, Polly, and a strange group of others (including a cab-pulling horse) find themselves magically dropped into a dark, empty space. Soon this place will grow into

Epilogue: "What Autumn Leaves Disclose"

Narnia (literally grow, with plants and trees and animals); but they don't know that yet, and it's so dark they can't see anything, so the general mood is one of hopelessness. Polly and Digory know they've made some bad mistakes, although blame should also be laid on wicked Uncle Andrew and the witch Jadis who escalated the whole thing. In any case, the word "crisis" perfectly describes this situation.

> "Crisis" in English comes from the Greek word [which is pronounced "kree-sis"]...And you know what it means? It means "decision." So, what's it telling you? The crisis is there to produce a decision, produce change.
>
> ...If you don't have resistance to your muscles, your muscles get weaker. In the same way, when you don't have spiritual resistance, you don't have resistance against your faith, your faith doesn't get stronger. You understand? In the same way, if you don't have resistance against your joy, your joy doesn't get stronger. It just gets dependent on things going up and down.
>
> (Jonathan Cahn, video)

I think Jonathan Cahn just handed us an outline of Charlotte Mason's teachings on character. Cahn says, "The crisis is there to produce a decision." Mason says, "The business of the will is to choose."

Cahn says, "When you don't have spiritual resistance, you don't have resistance against your faith, your faith doesn't get stronger." Mason says, "But, choice, the effort of decision, is a heavy labour, whether it be between two lovers or two gowns... We are zealous in choosing for others but shirk the responsibility of decisions for ourselves" (*Philosophy of Education*, pp. 133–134).

Cahn says, "[Your faith and joy get] dependent on things going up and down." Mason says, "Life is to such persons a series of casualties; things *happen* well or they happen ill, but they always happen...Shall we live this aimless, drifting life, or shall we take upon us the responsibility of our lives, and *will* as we go?" (*Ourselves Book 2*, p. 128).

The Greek word pronounced "kree-sis" can be used in medical contexts; in stories, we often read of a patient's fever reaching a "crisis," which means "decision time" in the body. "Kree-sis," or "Crisis," also relates to the evaluation made by a judge. Will he condemn the guilty or acquit the innocent? Think, perhaps, of a school principal dealing with a dozen children who seem to have been involved in a schoolyard fight. His responsibility in this "crisis" is to sort out those who started it, or those who happened to swing at somebody, from those who were just standing nearby and got marched in with the rest. The innocent ones go right back to class, a few of the others get a warning (and bandages), and then the one or two who caused the fight should get phone calls home or other punishment. Much depends on the person in charge getting all this right, and that's not a given, but it's what we hope for. And in the best outcome, we look for change: if not in the hearts of the fighters, at least perhaps in the circumstances leading up to the mess. Maybe more playground supervisors, maybe more balls or things to play with outside instead of hitting each other. Maybe moving somebody to another class, maybe parents curbing violent video games, maybe a school breakfast program so that children aren't so hangry by playground time.

The analogy can be applied to the case studies laid out in the first chapters of *Formation of Character*. Cahn says, "The crisis is there to produce a decision, produce change." There's always a bad situation, often one that has gone on way too long, and which erupts in a point of crisis. Little Guy has tantrums, Fred is irresponsible, Agnes has an attitude, and Mrs. Jumeau is sick in bed again. Somebody is forced to make a judgment call, a decision, which leads to change. They don't always get it right, at least not the first time, but even small changes add up. And the solutions almost always depend on recognizing the forces of resistance—against joy, against attention, against courage, against choice itself—and building up muscle, or Will, to fight those forces, along with the power of the Holy Spirit.

Polly and Digory and their crowd, waiting in the darkness, are about to witness that growth in a physical way, when Aslan comes to sing Narnia into existence. But in the meantime, one of the less-noticed characters decides it would be a good time for them all to sing.

> [The Cabby] struck up at once a harvest thanksgiving hymn, all about crops being "safely gathered in." It was not very suitable to a place which felt as if nothing had ever grown there since the beginning of time, but it was the one he could remember best. He had a fine voice and the children joined in; it was very cheering. (C. S. Lewis, *The*

Epilogue: "What Autumn Leaves Disclose"

Magician's Nephew)

This is our learning, our growth, our change. It is my story; it is your story, and your children's story. It could be the story of a dull-as-dishwater Sunday school, ready to be awakened. It could be about children who think they hate to read, or grownups who say they hate poetry, or nature walks, or singing, and then find out they don't. It could be about a literal garden, planted for your own family's needs or shared with a community. If you feel like "nothing has ever grown there since the beginning of time," there is always the possibility of restoration. Even in the driest, most neglected bits of ground, there can be life going on under our feet, as Jean-Henri Fabre reminded us.

This is why we are reminded to give thanks in everything, especially for the difficulties which can give us stronger roots and stems and leaves, and, eventually, better fruit.

Let's not depend on "things going up and down," but rather plant and tend and make and repair as faithfully as we can.

Let's "take upon us the responsibility of our lives, and *will* as we go." Let's sing what we remember, because it's very cheering.

And trust for the harvest.

"Cor ad Cor": A Postscript

I mentioned earlier that I had signed up for a class on faith and art. Our first homework assignment, given at the time I was completing this book, was to go out and notice something in nature, which seemed serendipitous. But how to create a response? I am not a painter or a sculptor. I don't weave or work with glass. Words are more my medium, but if even Malcolm Guite hesitated over writing an autumn poem, who am I to attempt one?

I have been re-reading Emily P. Freeman's *The Next Right Thing*, and today's chapter, read just before I went to the church to hand out groceries, was titled "Walk Into a Room." Can I walk in (anywhere) worrying less about my own welcome, and more about creating one for others? Knowing that I am free to belong in this place, in this story, allows me to attend to the needs of others, living "the common life, [not being stranded] in an inlet of individual culture" (*Formation of Character*, p. 302).

As I walked around the church building, I noticed an oak tree near the front door. I am nostalgic about oak trees, because I grew up surrounded by them, picking up acorns, waxing leaves, taking them for granted; but I also appreciate them because they are rarer where I live now, as in, "Look! An Oak!" Capitalized.

So, obeying the directive to look, and look again, I studied the oak tree in all its mid-autumnness. And this is what I noticed: some of the leaves had turned colour or even dropped, but others were still green. Some were so small and light green that they seemed newborn, even in October. All oak leaves, all on the same tree, but all different and all changing.

A couple of years ago, during Advent, we were (carefully) handed bits of coloured glass during a church service to take home and meditate on. After Christmas, the pieces were collected up again, and I believe they are now being worked into a piece of stained-glass art. The message? Like the leaves on the oak, we are all part of the picture, part of the story. We belong in the room, if we will only come in.

So, in an attempt to set aside my hesitant "I don't do poems," but also to avoid getting lost in a forest of autumnal clichés, I have written just one stanza in response to Guite's "And is it Not Enough?"

> I think it is enough that leaf by leaf
> Some palest green, some deeper hued, some gold
> Should find their place connected to the tree,
> And speak both childhood memories and grief,
> With glasslike hints and glints that can unfold
> And find that common life awake in me.

Epilogue: "What Autumn Leaves Disclose"

"Near the end of the book, she breaks off a thread and says, 'I think it's finished.

How can it be finished?'"

Bibliography

Alcott, Louisa May. *Little Women: Or, Meg, Jo, Beth and Amy.* Boston: Roberts Brothers, 1887/1880.

Alexander, Lloyd. *Taran Wanderer.* New York, NY: Dell, 1967.

Baxter, Jason M. *The Medieval Mind of C. S. Lewis: How Great Books Shaped a Great Mind.* IVP Academic, an imprint of InterVarsity Press, 2022.

Baxter, Jason M. *Why Literature Still Matters: Beauty after the Apocalypse.* 2nd edition, Cassiodorus Press, 2024.

Bell, Steve, & Malcolm Guite. "The Singing Bowl & Birth of a Song (Poem & Song)." YouTube video, September 13 2017. https://www.youtube.com/watch?v=swmiv9ERGCY&ab_channel=TheSteveBellYouTubeChannel

Bennett, Arnold. *How to Live On 24 Hours a Day.* Musson Book Co., 1910.

Bruce, Lynn. "A Magical Expansion: A study of Principle 12 of Charlotte Mason's 20 Principles." Retrieved from the AmblesideOnline website 09 October 2025. https://amblesideonline.org/art-magical-expansion

Cahn, Jonathan. "How to Turn Temptation into Victory." YouTube video, September 26, 2025. https://www.youtube.com/watch?v=oLR7dWUF5Yk

Cayley, David. *Northrop Frye in Conversation.* Toronto: House of Anansi Press, 1992.

Cholmondeley, Essex. *The Story of Charlotte Mason, 1842–1923.* Bristol, England: Lutterworth Press, 2021.

Bibliography

Clapham School. "The Liberal Art of Grammar (pt. 2)." Website article dated 13 December 2017. https://www.claphamschool.org/the-liberal-art-of-grammar/

Conkling, Hilda, "Tree-Toad," in *Poems by a Little Girl*. Frederick A. Stokes Company, 1920. Retrieved from AmblesideOnline website, October 9, 2025. https://amblesideonline.org/poet-conkling#04

Cooper, Susan. *The Gray King*. New York: Scholastic, 1975.

Dreher, Rod. *Living in Wonder: Finding Mystery and Meaning in a Secular Age*. Zondervan Books, 2024.

Edwards, Brad, and John Houmes. "Finding Meaning in a Fragmented World," with Jake Meador. *PostEverything*, 05 February 2025. Retrieved from Apple Podcasts 09 October 2025. https://podcasts.apple.com/cz/podcast/finding-meaning-in-a-fragmented-world-with-jake-meador/id1676174977?i=1000689264429

Eliot, T.S. *Four Quartets: The Centenary Edition (1888–1988)*. San Diego / New York / London: Harcourt Brace Jovanovich. Copyright 1943 by T.S. Eliot, copyright renewed 1971 by Esme Valerie Eliot.

Eliot, T. S. *Collected Poems 1909-1962*. London: Faber & Faber, 1974. ("The Love Song of J. Alfred Prufrock," "The Waste Land")

Emerson, Ralph Waldo, and Edward Waldo Emerson (ed.). *The complete works of Ralph Waldo Emerson: Lectures and biographical sketches [Vol. 10]*. Boston; New York: Houghton, Mifflin, 1903–1904.

Esolen, Anthony M. *Ten Ways to Destroy the Imagination of Your Child*. Wilmington, DE: ISI Books, 2010.

Fisher, Dorothy Canfield. *Understood Betsy*. New York, NY: Grosset & Dunlap, 1917.

Freeman, Emily P. *The Next Right Thing: A Simple, Soulful Practice for*

Making Life Decisions. Revell, 2019.

Frye, Northrop. *The Educated Imagination*. Toronto: Canadian Broadcasting Corporation, 1963.

Gardner, Anthony. "Somerset: Why Tom loved the last word." *Daily Telegraph*, 4 September 2002. Retrieved from Anthony Gardner's website 09 October 2025.
https://www.anthonygardner.co.uk/travel_writing/east_coker.html

Gardner, Helen. *The Art of T.S. Eliot*. E.P. Dutton & Co., 1959.

Glass, Karen. *In Vital Harmony: Charlotte Mason and the Natural Laws of Education*. N.p., 2019.

Goudge, Elizabeth. *Pilgrim's Inn*. Peabody, MA: Hendrickson Publishers Marketing, LLC, 2013. (Published in London as *The Herb of Grace*, 1948).

Green, Keith, with Todd Fishkind and Randy Stonehill. "Your Love Broke Through," on the album *For Him Who Has Ears to Hear*, released 1977 by Sparrow Records.

Guite, Malcolm. "'And Is It Not Enough?' My own Autumn poem." YouTube video, 17 September 2025.
https://www.youtube.com/watch?v=HdO31JoWuJU

Guite, Malcolm. "The Soul's Blood" in *After Prayer: New Sonnets and Other poems*. London: Canterbury Press, 2019.

Hamilton, Edith. *Mythology*. Grand Central Publishing, 2011.

Haskell, Arlo. "A Great Wonder: Richard Wilbur in Conversation." Posted on *Poets.org*, 28 February 2011. Retrieved 09 October 2025.
https://poets.org/text/great-wonder-richard-wilbur-conversation

Hawthorne, Nathaniel. *A Wonder Book for Girls & Boys,* Illustrated

Bibliography

by Walter Crane. Oxford University Press, 1893.

Hawthorne, Nathaniel. *Tanglewood Tales*. Illustrated by Milo Winter, Windermere series, Rand McNally, 1913.

Hazlitt, William. "On Poetry in General," in *The Collected Works of William Hazlitt*, edited by A. R. Waller and Arnold Glover, with an introduction by W. E. Henley. London: J. M. Dent & Co., 1902.

Jacobs, Alan. *The Narnian: The Life and Imagination of C.S. Lewis*. HarperCollins, 2005.

Jacobs, Alan. "The Truth in View" on *The Homebound Symphony*. Blog post of 11 August 2025. Retrieved 9 October 2025. https://blog.ayjay.org/the-truth-in-view/

Jellema, Rod. "Poems Should Stay Across the Street from the Church," first published in *Christianity Today* (1976). Included in *The Christian Imagination: Essays on Literature and the Arts*, edited by Leland Ryken, Baker Book House Company, 1981.

Karon, Jan. *Light from Heaven*. Penguin Books, 2005.

Karon, Jan. *To Be Where You Are*. New York, NY: G.P. Putnam's Sons, 2017.

Keary, Annie, and Eliza Keary. *The Heroes of Asgard: Tales from Scandinavian Mythology*. London: Macmillan, 1908.

Kingsley, Charles. *Madam How and Lady Why, or, First Lessons in Earth Lore for Children*. New York: The Macmillan Company, 1901.

Kirk, Russell. *Eliot and His Age: TS Eliot's Moral Imagination in the Twentieth Century*. ISI Books, 1984.

Lewis, C. S. *The Last Battle*. London: The Bodley Head, 1956.

Lewis, C. S. *The Magician's Nephew*. London: The Bodley Head, 1955.

Lewis, C. S. *Out of the Silent Planet*. London: John Lane, The Bodley Head, 1938.

Lewis, C. S. *A Preface to Paradise Lost*. Oxford University Press, 1942.

Lewis, C. S., and Walter Hooper. *Present Concerns*. Fount, 1986. ("On Living in an Atomic Age")

Lewis, C. S. *Till We Have Faces*. London: Geoffrey Bles, 1956.

Lewis C. S. "The Weight of Glory," in *The Weight of Glory and Other Addresses*. New York: HarperCollins, 2001.

Lewis, C. S. *Voyage of the Dawn Treader*. London: Geoffrey Bles, 1955.

Lowry, Lois. *A Summer to Die*. Houghton Mifflin, 1977.

Markos, Louis. *The Myth Made Fact: Reading Greek and Roman Mythology Through Christian Eyes*. Classical Academic Press, 2020.

Mason, Charlotte M. *Formation of Character*. Vol. 5 of *The Original Home Schooling Series*. Wheaton, IL: Tyndale House, 1989. Originally published 1906 as *Some Studies in the Formation of Character* by Kegan Paul, Trench, Trubner and Co., Ltd. (London). Page references are to the 1989 edition.

Mason, Charlotte M. *Ourselves*. Vol. 4 of *The Original Home Schooling Series*. Wheaton, IL: Tyndale House, 1989. Originally published 1905 by Kegan Paul, Trench, Trubner and Co., Ltd. (London). Page references are to the 1989 edition.

Mason, Charlotte M. *Parents and Children*. Vol. 2 of *The Original Home Schooling Series*. Wheaton, IL: Tyndale House, 1989. Originally published 1904 by Kegan Paul, Trench, Trubner and Co., Ltd. (London). Page references are to the 1989 edition.

Bibliography

Mason, Charlotte M. *A Philosophy of Education.* Vol. 6 of *The Original Home Schooling Series.* Wheaton, IL: Tyndale House, 1989. Originally published 1925 as *An Essay Towards a Philosophy of Education* by Kegan Paul, Trench, Trubner and Co., Ltd. (London). Page references are to the 1989 edition.

Mason, Charlotte M. *School Education.* Vol. 3 of *The Original Home Schooling Series.* Wheaton, IL: Tyndale House, 1989. Originally published 1907 by Kegan Paul, Trench, Trubner and Co., Ltd. (London). Page references are to the 1989 edition.

McGilchrist, Iain. *The Matter with Things: Our Brains, Our Delusions, and the Unmaking of the World.* Perspectiva Press, 2021.

Millay, Edna St. Vincent. "God's World." Retrieved from Poetry Foundation Website.
https://www.poetryfoundation.org/poems/51862/gods-world

Oliver, Mary. *Devotions: The Selected Poems of Mary Oliver.* Penguin Press, an imprint of Penguin Random House LLC, 2017. ("The summer day")

Paterson, Katherine. *Gates of Excellence: On Reading and Writing Books for Children.* Dutton/Lodestar, 1981

Phillips, J. B., with an introduction by C. S. Lewis. *Letters to Young Churches: A Translation of the New Testament Epistles.* London: Collins, 1947.

Piper, John. "Clyde Kilby's Resolutions for Mental Health and for Staying Alive to God in Nature." Posted on DesiringGod.org, 27 August 1990. Retrieved 09 October 2025.
https://www.desiringgod.org/articles/clyde-kilbys-resolutions-for-mental-health-and-for-staying-alive-to-god-in-nature

Plutarch & North, Thomas (trans.) *Lives of the Noble Grecians and Romans.* London: Dent, 1894/5.

Potter, Beatrix. *The Tale of Peter Rabbit*. Frederick Warne, 1902.

Renault, Mary. *The Mask of Apollo*. Pantheon Books, 1966.

Ruef, Kerry. *The Private Eye Teacher Guide—(5X) Looking / Thinking by Analogy*. Can be purchased through The Private Eye website, https://www.theprivateeyestore.com/.

Spurgeon, Charles Haddon. "The Pity of the Lord—The Comfort of the Afflicted," Sermon No. 1845. It is found in *Spurgeon's Sermons Volume 31: 1885*, published by Christian Classics Ethereal Library, Grand Rapids, MI. Retrieved from the CCE website 09 October 2025. https://ccel.org/ccel/s/spurgeon/sermons31/cache/sermons31.pdf

The Golden Girls [T.V. Series]. Created by Susan Harris, Touchstone Television, 1985–1992.

Thompson, Francis. "The Hound of Heaven." Retrieved from the Hound of Heaven website, 10 October 2025.
https://www.houndofheaven.com/poem

Time to Run [Film]. Produced by the Billy Graham Evangelistic Association, 1973.

Toy Story [Film]. Directed by John Lasseter. Pixar Animation Studios, Walt Disney Pictures, 1995.

Toy Story 2 [Film]. Directed by John Lasseter. Pixar Animation Studios, Walt Disney Pictures, 2005.

Toy Story 3 [Film]. Directed by Lee Unkrich. Pixar Animation Studios, Walt Disney Pictures, 2010.

Vencel, Brandy. "Ep. 23: Learning How to Live." Transcript of *Aftercast*, Episode 23, published on *Afterthoughts*, 13 December 2018. Retrieved 06 October 2025.
https://afterthoughtsblog.net/2018/12/aftercast-learning-live-transcript.html/.

Bibliography

White, Anne E. *Offering Ourselves: A Lenten Journey with Charlotte Mason*. N.p., 2023.

White, Anne E. *The Practical Plutarch*. N.p., 2021.

Wilbur, Richard. Collected *Poems 1943-2004*. New York: Houghton Mifflin Harcourt Publishing Company, 2004. ("Lying")

Williams, Paul. "The Challenge of Writing 'Rainbow Connection' for Kermit." YouTube video posted by Bullseye With Jesse Thorn. https://www.youtube.com/shorts/QNktuQoWLcE.

Yancey, Philip. "Why I Write." Blog post dated June 2016. https://philipyancey.com/why-i-write/ Retrieved 06 October 2025.

Parents' Review Articles

These articles may be read on the AmblesideOnline website.

Mason, Charlotte (1890/91). A new educational departure. *Parents' Review, 1*, pp. 69–74.

Ambler, "Miss M." (1901). "Plutarch's lives" as affording some education as a citizen. *Parents' Review, 12*, 521–527.

Parish, "Miss E. A. [Ellen]". (1914). Imagination as a powerful factor in a well-balanced mind. *Parents' Review, 25 "No. 5"*, pp. 379–390.

www.ingramcontent.com/pod-product-compliance
Lightning Source LLC
Chambersburg PA
CBHW060847050426
42453CB00008B/868